GOVERNMENT AND POLITICS
IN LATIN AMERICA

STUDIES IN
POLITICAL
SCIENCE

Government and Politics
in Latin America

R. A. GOMEZ
University of Arizona

RANDOM HOUSE / NEW YORK

CONTENTS

CHAPTER ONE

The Iberian Heritage

The foundations of Latin American government were laid centuries ago by a dedicated group of men from the Iberian peninsula.* The motivations, aspirations, and character of these men formed the spirit of the colonial ventures, and later, this spirit was deeply imbedded in the administrators of a long colonial period and in the leaders of modern Latin American republics. Much of Latin American government in the mid-twentieth century appears quite in keeping with the spirit of Spain in the mid-sixteenth century.

The colonies of the area we now refer to as Latin America were under continuously rigid administration by the mother country for approximately three hundred years. The effect of this extended period, although much elabo-

* The terms "Iberian" and "Spanish" are used frequently in these pages. Simplicity demands that the French origin of Haiti not be given special recognition in all these cases.

rated and emphasized in all histories of the area, must nevertheless be brought to the fore in each successive attempt to understand Latin American affairs. The appreciation of this effect can first be encouraged by certain meaningful references to the length of time involved. For example, it may be helpful to reflect that the entire history of the United States from the adoption of the Constitution covers a period of only one-hundred and seventy years. Or, to make a comparison perhaps more pertinent, the period of the full life of the United States from the first substantial colonial ventures to the present time closely approximates the three-hundred-year period we are trying to appreciate.

Still more meaningful is the time element expressed in terms of institutional development. During those three hundred years of colonial administration in Latin America, Western political institutions evolved from absolute monarchy to representative government; the factor of accountability was brought into institutional form. Those three hundred years witnessed, for example, the significant events in the development of the present British parliamentary democracy—constitutional monarchy under the domination of popular and representative instruments. In France, during this period, in an application of greater abruptness, essentially the same new forces in the political order sheared away the *ancien régime* and, in the process, contributed ideological expression invaluable for the spirit of man. In the northern latitudes of the New World, the United States formed and consolidated a system that combined the time-tested institutions of British origin with the freshness and innovation of the New World environment. In all three revolutions—the heritage of the Enlightenment and preceding developments—there was to be observed the force, then narrowly applied, that by our own time has become massive in nature—popular government.

During this whole period of exciting development, the colonies of Latin America remained under a colonial system that did not favor participation in the evolution of

European thought and institutions. To be sure, some colonists partook of the new spirit, but they were compelled to guard their thinking carefully and they had no direct experience in the institutions born of these ideas.[1]

The Spirit of Expansion

The great adventure that took Europeans to the New World was the result of a general adventurousness that entered European life toward the end of the Middle Ages. Feudalism was beginning to move timidly into new social arrangements that eventually solidified into the nation-state. Feudalism had relied upon an elaborate series of compacts among various orders of kings, lords, and lesser ranks. It was a way of life based upon a very complicated network of property-holding relationships. In return for the privileges of property-holding, loyalty and service were promised. The Church was a powerful participant in the system and, indeed, for a great part of the Middle Ages, dominated all of life. It was the world depicted in St. Augustine's *City of God* and later more carefully drawn into a divinely inspired cosmic unity in the work of St. Thomas Aquinas. Life on earth was largely viewed as a preparatory exercise for a possible heavenly life beyond the celestial portal of the cosmic community. In social terms, this meant a rigid and functional society composed of a few privileged spiritual and temporal princes, a second rank of lesser nobles, a group of honored and storied military orders, and finally a vast sea of common people who lived chiefly for satisfaction promised beyond the celestial portal of the *City*.

At some time in the late Middle Ages the new spirit appeared, at first in isolated fashion; even at its height, it was not observable at the same intensity in any two regions of Europe. It was evident, however, that there was everywhere to some degree, and very spiritedly indeed in some places, a new eagerness for inquiry into science and man. An optimism and energy centered upon individual initiative brought forward a large number of gifted men motivated by a new impetus. The individual was increasing in value. He began relating himself more personally to the world around him; he showed some interest in contemplating earthly accomplishment; humanism in art and thought found expression. Not even the Church escaped this assault. In the fifteenth and sixteenth centuries a number of churchmen objected to papal domination and sought reforms in the direction of more representative organization of the hierarchy. The writings of some dissenting churchmen contain ideas that were later applied in a wider secular meaning—representation, the contract as a foundation for authority, and even the right of revolt. Very broadly viewed, all of this activity was the Renaissance, an upsurge of energies of incalculable consequences for the future.

Accompanying all of the aforementioned movements and ideas was an increasing emphasis on trade. The earlier phases of modern capitalism and the industrial revolution were evident in the towns, particularly those favorably located on water and land routes. A rising merchant class was amassing fortunes by supplying luxuries for gold and other easily negotiable forms of wealth. Although scornful at first of trade as a livelihood, kings and nobles eventually became dependent upon the medium of exchange that was rapidly circulating ever more widely. International relationships in the formative stage of the nation-state found gold a convenient expediter. National policy came to be formed around a preoccupation with the discovery and storage of gold and other precious minerals. As a corollary interest, an active search for raw materials to feed growing industries took nations into the quest for colonies. The desire for luxury commodities—chiefly silk finery and spices—had accounted for a long time for a thriving trade with the Orient. Goods were transported by land and sea over the long route from Asia to the Mediterranean, where the merchants distributed them to the European markets. However, by the fifteenth century, the Moslem Turks had placed themselves in control along the overland routes and therefore blocked this trade. The discovery of new water routes to the Orient became the object of feverish activity among the maritime nations of Europe. Thus, in addition to a certain restlessness of spirit, an economic motive entered the picture.

In Spain, where much of the general awakening had little effect, there was nevertheless a considerable energy for expansion by reason of an internal situation, in addition to the normal compulsions of monarchy in international affairs, that forged the unconquerable spirit of the *conquistadores* and launched Spain's era of glory. For centuries Spaniards had been engaged in a crusade against Moorish occupation, an occupation dating from the eighth century. Therefore, at the time that the Protestant Reformation was laying hold of a good part of Europe, Spaniards were zealously carrying the Church's banners into battle against the infidel and creating a deeper loyalty to the Church. Spanish warriors took up the Cross and intensified the institution that was being weakened elsewhere.

To understand the vigor and dedication of the *conquistadores* in the New World, one must appreciate the zeal and the discipline that was generated by a triumphant crusade on the Iberian peninsula. In the very year that Columbus sailed for the new world, the last of the Moors were expelled from Spain. The momentum carried into the New World.

Discovery and Conquest

Columbus undertook the venture to the Indies by contract with the Crown.[2] In return for assistance with ships and provisions and the promise of titles and personal gain, Columbus agreed to certain terms to benefit his sponsors. Specifically, he was granted the office of admiral, which was to pass on to his heirs; he was to be viceroy and governor of lands claimed for the Crown; he was to have the power of appointment of lesser officials; and he was to be granted a priority in the financing of future ventures. The Crown was to have sovereignty over lands claimed and to receive one-tenth of the pearls, precious stones, and spices. Although varying in details, this contractual approach was followed during the years of discovery through the sixteenth century.

Many of the conquerors were granted the title of *adelantado*,[3] an office traceable as far back as tenth-century Spain. The *adelantado* was an official "put forward" in the King's place and representing him in remote parts of the realm. Columbus appears not to have had this title, because the first one on record was conferred on his brother Bartholomew. Beginning in 1512, a succession of *adelantados* appears with royal commissions. Many were titles promised if performance warranted it, although others were conferred outright before the venture was undertaken. It has been concluded that some 70 individuals contracted with the Crown during the period of exploration and conquest; of these, less than half were given the title of *adelantado*, among them Balboa, Pizarro, Ponce de León, Mendoza, Orellana, Oñate, and Velásquez. Oñate's appears to have been the last one granted—in the year 1600. The renowned Cortes was never given the title, apparently, although he held the titles of governor and captain-general.

The explorer sometimes furnished the expenses of the venture; but in any event, a contract, or *capitulación*, was always drawn up. In addition to the agreements about titles for the explorers and the rights of the Crown to certain wealth, a typical *capitulación* set forth the nature of the venture (discovery, exploration, pacification of Indians, for example), made clear the responsibility of the *adelantado* for carrying the Faith to the natives (including the occasional provision that two priests must accompany the expedition), provided for land distribution, and the like.[4]

Whether or not the explorer held the title of *adelantado*, all these men were in fact agents of the Crown, and we are accustomed to refer to them collectively as the *con-*

quistadores. The incredible exploits of many of them
hardly need narration here. Lord Bryce referred to them
as "men of extraordinary audacity and energy," the like
of which had not been seen since "the Norsemen of the
tenth century and their children, the Normans of the
eleventh." [5] Some of their accomplishments stir the imagination and appear heroic beyond any adequate description.
The feats of the Spanish *conquistador* may well be the last
stand of the medieval knight. They were in the tradition
of storied knights of the years of the expulsion of the
Moors. Undoubtedly they believed themselves to be divinely
ordained with the mission of carrying the Faith and the
glory of Spain to the corners of the earth; and, at the same
time, they sought eagerly and without fear of tremendous
sacrifice the fulfillment of their own deeply etched sense
of honor and pride. It should be noted, however, that a
feverish search for the things of wealth and power was
involved. Frequently, greed and callous disregard for the
natives accompanied their search. Individualism was being
fulfilled under conditions that offered few restraints. The
era has been portrayed as "a rebel world that was born
under the auspices of absolutism, which in giving flight to
individualism was in conflict with the very feudalism
from which it was derived." [6]

The Crown Strengthens Its Position

After the discovery and early conquests in the New World,
the Crown took steps to insure that control of the Indies
should be properly secured. The *conquistadores* had served
a purpose that must now be turned to advantage. Furthermore, there were evidences that some of the conquerors
(particularly Cortes) considered themselves independent of
the Crown or, at least, were taking advantage of distance
to act so. And even before, during the Columbus years, the
Crown had seen the necessity of interfering by sending an
official to impose a stronger grip on the colonies. (And
thus was commenced the practice of *visita,* by which the

Crown conducted investigations throughout the colonial period.) After a time a system was implanted in the Indies that characterized the colonial administration for the greater part of three hundred years.

This centralization of control paralleled a movement that was taking place in Spain itself. Much earlier, during the long conflict with the Moors, Spain was considerably decentralized in a loose system consisting of strong and independent nobles who reigned over their own towns. In many cases towns were granted special charters of autonomy in return for assistance against the Moors or for keeping the peace. The Crown often incorporated such towns to create friends who could offset the power of unfriendly nobles. Very slowly during the twelfth and thirteenth centuries, and more rapidly through the fifteenth century, the kingdoms of Castile and Aragon grew in power at the expense of many such independent entities until by the time of Isabella and Ferdinand much of Spain was centralized. The offices and practices involved in this centralization were employed to strengthen the Crown in the Indies.

By the time of Charles I (1516-1556), the monarchy could be said to be centralized and absolute. The *cortes,* which was a legislative body like the early form of the British parliament and which, as the sounding board for the localities and regions of Spain, had formerly been a vigorous political entity, became clearly subordinate to the king. The ministers and councils privy to the king replaced the parliamentary organization.

In the Indies, therefore, occurred changes that reflected these events in Spain. However, as will be noted later, sheer distance has a way of reducing the effects of even the strongest system.

The Portuguese in Brazil

The Portuguese occupation of the bulge of modern South America came about with much less drama. There was no haste on the part of the Portuguese to occupy and explore their share of the New World. When word came of the riches being realized by the Spaniards, somewhat more attention was paid to the possibilities, but it was not until 1532 that the first formal settlement by royal grant was made. This was carried out under the leadership of the first royal governor, Martim Affonso de Souza. This royally sponsored settlement was at São Vicente, in the area now known as the Brazilian state of São Paolo.

As Spain employed techniques and offices based on earlier experience, so too the Portuguese employed a system first applied in earlier European colonial enterprises. However, in practice, no substantial centralization was exercised until the latter half of the seventeenth century. Portuguese officials in the New World were granted considerable freedom to act as the situation warranted; accordingly, a rather easy-going atmosphere prevailed.

The Portuguese conquest was not, of course, carried out on as vast a scale as the Spanish conquest. Nor was the Portuguese effort motivated by as much crusading or marauding zeal.

The Colonial Heritage

The colonial system left deeply ingrained traditions that were to affect, immediately, the national organizational problems and, thereafter, the operation of these national schemes continuously down to our time. In the following paragraphs, the major impacts of this system will be briefly described. It will be noted that, in almost every particular, there is substantial contrast to the North American colonial experience.

Authoritarianism. A reflection of the Spain of its day, the colonial system featured an authoritarian structure in all respects.[7] The entire Indies venture was considered a personal possession of the Crown. The Crown employed a few advisory councils—the Council of the Indies in particular—to expedite this administrative problem. The New World, after the spread of the system to its fullest extent, consisted of a number of kingdoms headed by viceroys, who in turn were responsible for lesser jurisdictions under the control of governors and other titled officials. In frontier areas, captaincies-general were created with the same pattern in mind but with less prestige and responsibility. In a pattern of centralization down to the municipal level, the Crown, through detailed legislation, attempted to exercise sweeping authority. In addition to the hierarchy of essentially executive officials, there were *audiencias,* councils of judicial and administrative duties. These *audiencias* brought into the colonial scheme a method of independent check upon the rest of the system.[8]

There was very little popular participation in the political process. Whatever slight amount there was occurred at the local level, where occasionally there were "town meetings" in the sense that the *cabildo,* comparable to the modern city council in structure but not in manner of selection, opened up its meetings to some "public" participation.[9] These stand in sharp contrast to town meetings as later employed in the United States in that the members of the *cabildo* were not necessarily elective officials and the invited participants were in no position to compel attention to their views. It is to be noted, however, that the *cabildos* of a number of colonial cities formed the spearhead of independence movements.

Prestige of the Military. In the circle of prestige in the colonial system stood the military officers. They had inherited the mantle of the medieval military orders who had led the expulsion of the Moors and who later led the small forces of conquest in the New World. The military function was indeed important to the maintenance of the whole colonial structure. Viceroys and captains-general were military commanders as well as civil leaders. Never has a system been based on such dependence upon loyalty, for the few organized forces were responsible for vast areas, within some of which were irrepressible Indian tribes. The pride of the military was sustained by the New World system. It was inevitable that the military should remain powerful in the political struggles of the nineteenth and twentieth centuries.

Personalism. The authoritarian system employed in the Indies and the rarefied atmosphere of colonial officialdom contributed greatly to an already deeply etched sense of honor, pride, and self-centeredness. The few who ruled ritualized these qualities into the culture, particularly in the capital cities.

Even more deeply involved in this *personalismo* was a cultural heritage, centuries old, from the Iberian peninsula, which might be said to extend to all the colonists, regardless of status in the power structure. As far back as Roman days, the Iberians have been regarded as fiercely individualistic and proud. This is a political fact of the greatest significance in modern Latin American life, as will be seen in later pages.

The Church.[10] As indicated earlier, the Spanish Church was the very heart of counter-reformation strength. Therefore, it was very closely engaged in the colonial system, which was in theory justified as necessary to disseminate the Faith. The Church was as much a ministry of the Crown as the normal agencies of administration; the fact that it had, to some degree, its separate status as an arm of the Roman Catholic hierarchy elevated it, if anything, in the whole scheme.

The colonial system was very substantially affected by the power of the Church. It managed the moral and literary spheres and exercised considerable censorship over both throughout the whole colonial period. In addition, it was a property owner of considerable stature, and it administered the educational and welfare institutions. Hardly an activity in colonial society escaped its influence.

Socio-economic Order. The authoritarian arrangement of power and the essentially exploitive nature of the economic order led the colonial system inevitably into a land-tenure system characterized by enormous holdings in the hands of the few who were favored by the Crown. Large land grants were the price paid by the Crown for the settlement and exploitation of the New World. The fact that this had none of the character of the family-farm enterprise as in colonial North America was of incalculable effect on the future of Latin American economic systems as well as on the social order. Very little opportunity was presented for the development of attitudes and aspirations identifiable with "social mobility." No middle class emerged during the colonial period, and, indeed, much of Latin America is still lacking in this modern social phenomenon so closely related to abundant economic systems. Thus, the colonial period brought forth a socio-economic order based on scarcity.

Law.[11] Throughout the colonial period an enormous amount of legislation was passed for the management of the Indies. The Laws of the Indies reached downward in great detail and attempted to circumscribe the whole societal activity. This was in effect a superimposition of special law over the old codes applied on the peninsula. Often confusion occurred over which law should be applied in specific instances, because a certain amount of contradiction, at least in interpretation, was inevitable. The officials in the Indies were allowed to question the applicability of new legislation and to send back to Spain the reasons for such delay; if the request was turned down, the law, perhaps after several years lapse of time, would then go into effect. The great distance between the source of law and its application obviously created attitudes of noncompliance that were, over the centuries, regarded as part of the administrative process.

Thus, the colonial heritage with respect to law offered, in addition to the formalism of the continental tradition,

two significant factors: a disposition to accept law cover-
ing considerable detail in the life of the society, and a
tendency among those in power to regard the law as a
manipulative commodity.

Concessionary View of Public Office. Because, in the
authoritarian structure, holders of office felt little responsibility to the people, public offices were regarded
either as labels of prestige or, as at the local level, property
rights that were negotiable assets, for the sale of such
offices was common. In either case, there was a decided
tendency to view public posts as concessions that the con-
cessionaires were expected to exploit to their advantage.
The fact that not all invariably operated in this fashion—
and many indeed were the conscientious office holders—
does not detract from the tendency broadly demonstrated.
The concessionary view clings determinedly to office-
holding in Latin America today.

Incipient Nationalisms. Although the colonial venture was
strongly characterized by cultural uniformity, nevertheless
the vastness of the area administered inevitably generated
much insularity. Communications over such a vast area,
extending from the Horn into a very great portion of the
present western United States, was of course difficult. Thus,
over generations and indeed centuries, an identification
with a reasonably encompassable area arose; some of the
smaller jurisdictions, such as the *audiencia,* were regarded
as national areas, or as "kingdoms" with separate status
with respect to the Crown.[12]

The Collective Impact of the Colonial Experience. Unlike
the English colonies of North America, the Latin American colonies came forward into the nineteenth century
without the substance necessary to move immediately into
effective representative government. The institutions of
consent were almost entirely absent. Government was
certainly not going to be instituted in the tradition of

laissez-faire, as was characteristic of early nineteenth-century liberalism. Nationalism prevented any consolidation, as in the form of confederation. Therefore, the voids in each case were inevitably filled by military leadership. When the independence movement against Spain gained headway, a curious combination of authoritarianism and modern republican idealism was the result.

Independence and the Formation of Republicanism

The Latin American colonies of Spanish origin revolted and ultimately won independence after scattered and prolonged wars lasting from 1808 to 1826. The Wars for Independence constitute one of the substantial revolutions of modern times; fought in the name of the same ideals and aspirations that accompanied the American and French revolutions, the revolution was the last one fought by virtue of the impetus of the Revolutionary Age.

Intellectual Ferment. The making of modern revolutions, particularly in the early stages, is largely in the hands of the intellectuals and the power elite, who can articulate to the point necessary to arouse mass support.[13] In Latin America, a number of well-educated *creoles* provided this leadership. As examples, they had the two exciting emancipations that had occurred but a few decades earlier in North America and France and, to some extent, the still earlier English revolution that had generated so much brilliant revolutionary language. Although the Church exercised strict censorship over political literature of this type, a brisk business developed in the smuggling of banned works into some of the colonies. Many young *creoles* traveled in Europe and the United States and were thus able to read widely in such works and perhaps also to smuggle them into their countries. Translations were circulated of some of the stirring literature of revolution and natural rights, such as Nariño's translation of the Declaration of the Rights of Man and of the Citizen.

Francisco Miranda, a *creole* from Carácas, spent years traveling in Europe and the United States as an agent for the cause of separation, during which time he maintained continuous correspondence with leaders in the colonies.[14]

A typical revolutionary was Mariano Moreno of Buenos Aires.[15] He was educated at the University of San Francisco Xavier at Chuquisaca, which was considered the intellectual fountain of South America. Here were to be found revolutionist literature and other forbidden books. Moreno became familiar with Montesquieu, Locke, Rousseau, Jovellanos, the Encyclopedists, Adam Smith, and Tom Paine. Upon the seizure of the Spanish throne by Napoleonic forces, Moreno became one of the secretaries of the *junta* set up in Buenos Aires. Furthermore, in 1810, he founded the *Gaceta de Buenos Aires* and was able to disseminate his ideas widely through that medium.

The Cabildos. It was the *cabildo,* the municipal instrumentality of the colonial system, that furnished the impetus for revolt. This was a natural source of action since it was the only institution of the system with which the *creoles* could identify themselves, higher institutions in the system being manned only by *peninsulares* (those born in Spain).

The *cabildos* became revolutionary *juntas* professing loyalty to the deposed King Ferdinand VII. Later, when the restoration of Ferdinand was accomplished, the momentum for separation had become too strong to be opposed. In 1810, the *cabildos* of Carácas, Buenos Aires, New Granada, and Santiago de Chile declared independence; in the north, Mexico City was the center of revolt under the leadership of the central *junta* at Seville.

The Pains of National Organization. The great Argentine statesman Domingo Sarmiento once wrote: "Would that a people could be free by the same sort of *ad hominem* arguments that can bring about independence!" [16] This lament sums up very well the problems encountered in setting up the Latin American republics following the Wars for Independence.

After 1831, the date of the break-up of Great Colombia, 11 independent states were in existence: Mexico, The United Provinces of Central America, Colombia, Venezuela, Ecuador, Peru, Bolivia, Chile, Paraguay, Argentina, and Uruguay. Almost all were nearly identical with old colonial jurisdictions; Uruguay may be said to have split off unnaturally from a larger jurisdiction, but even it had been known as the *Banda Oriental,* relative to the La Plata region.

Ideas on organization ranged through virtually all the political spectrum, from monarchy to the freest sort of democratic republic. But strong in the center of the pattern of thought was a belief that the new states were not ready for the fulfillment of revolutionary ideals. Bolívar, whose own thought vacillated on the question, was basically convinced through it all that some attention should be given to an authoritarian foundation; among other institutions, he suggested life presidencies and dictatorships.[17] He is said to have remarked that "the new States of America, once Spanish, need kings with the title of President." [18] Monteagudo, the Argentine journalist, who favored monarchy, wrote that they were "not able to be as free as those who were born in that classic land, England, . . . nor as free as the democrats of North America." [19]

Despite the variety of notions about organization, one type of leader and source of power was available to all—the military commander. For many decades a large part of Latin America was in fact dominated by the military leader, the *caudillo,* who often was able to call upon the loyalty of large bands of followers.[20] All the first chiefs of state were military heroes—Itúrbide in Mexico, O'Higgins in Chile, Rivadavia in Argentina, Bolívar in New Granada, and many others. The situation was further complicated by internal skirmishes for national power among several *caudillos,* as in Argentina and Mexico. The *caudillos* were of many types. Some genuinely sought power as a temporary bridge over which organization of the new republic might pass quickly; some were cruel tyrants without appreciation of any idealistic side of the matter; some were educated *creoles* with a high regard for honor and intellect; some were ignorant *mestizos* or Indians who prized only strength and loyalty. In many parts of Latin America, *caudillismo* of this early variety reigned for many decades; violence and anarchy were widespread. Indeed, it may be said that the *caudillo* competition in some countries did not cease until the 1920's (as in Mexico).

Constitutions. If the keynote for the exercise of power was *caudillismo,* the architectural lines of the state were rational and idealistic. As they appeared in the form of written constitutions, they invariably depicted the fullest operation of the republican form of government. These constitutions showed the influence of the United States, France, and to some extent the Spanish Constitution of 1812. The French and North American fundamental laws were especially appealing as models because they embodied successful formulae for the institutionalization of revolution.

CHAPTER TWO

Constitutions and

General Structure

In the preceding chapter, suggestions were made concerning the influences at work among the newly-formed Latin American states in the early decades of the nineteenth century. Revolutionary doctrines from abroad had laid hold of the imaginations; change was the spirit of the day. Possessing a combination of legalism, from their own experience, and the constitutionalism of the United States and France, by adoption, the designers of these states turned to the drafting of constitutions that would demonstrate both these influences.[1] These constitutions drew heavily upon the natural-rights concept and the structural elements found in prominent constitutions of the day. Ideas were everywhere more plentiful than the results of experience. Principle rather than precedent flavored the approach. The new constitutions were strongly disposed to enshrine the abstract. They tended to describe goals, not intrenched institutions.

Constitutions and Their Creation

One of the most widely observed characteristics of Latin American government is the disposition to create constitutions with considerable frequency. Constitutional assemblies dot the pages of the histories of the republics. To the North American this is particularly bewildering. It is contradictory to his long-entertained notions about constitutions—notions that center around the feeling that a constitution is fundamental law, coming from the deep springs of a nation's experience. A constitution appears to him the very symbol of stability and continuity. To be sure, he loads some of his state constitutions with ephemeral material, but he views this as change on the periphery and not at the core; and, in any event, he is very disinclined to adopt wholly new or even substantially revised constitutions.

Some of the Latin American republics have provided new constitutions more than 20 times during their brief histories. Some of the republics most frequently drafting new constitutions are (roughly in descending order) Venezuela, the Dominican Republic, Peru, Bolivia, Ecuador, Haiti, El Salvador, and Honduras. Exact numbers are somewhat misleading since many so-called new constitutions have been, in reality, amended versions of older ones. But they are invariably represented as new by a new and zealous regime. In the period since the end of World War II, most of the republics have come forth with at least one new constitution.

As is consistent with modern constitution-making, Latin American constitutions are quite lengthy. (In this they are similar to many of the state constitutions in the United States.) The main reason for this length is a decided preoccupation with modern socio-economic problems, which are treated remedially in very long sections. The Mexican Constitution of 1917 (still in force) is a good deal longer than that of the United States, primarily because of the great attention to rights, the property relationships, and other examples of increasing emphasis on socio-economic improvement and economic nationalism. Possibly the longest constitution in Latin American experience was the Cuban Constitution of 1940, which dealt with the afore-mentioned matters in considerable detail and, in addition, was rather longer in such other respects as the structure of government.

The process of constitutional amendment varies from republic to republic. A very common method is simply by vote of congress, perhaps by a two-thirds majority. There is a tendency therefore to regard the constituent power (as it is called in the United States) as merely a legislative power with—admittedly—a greater importance. In some republics, the president is presented with an opportunity to object, although in each case his objection may be overridden. A few provide for constitutional conventions following a specified vote of approval in the congress. Generally speaking, the congress provides the constitutional medium through which the governing group may act by the pressure of presidential leadership.

Constituent Assemblies. Constitutions are normally created by constituent assemblies or congresses. These have become a very familiar part of the Latin American scene. Although occasionally called by virtue of a constitutional procedure, more often they are the result of such extraconstitutional situations as *coup d'état*. Following a *coup* there will generally be a desire on the part of the new regime to rewrite, or perhaps reintroduce under new sponsorship, the fundamental basis for the state. A constituent assembly is accordingly convened, perhaps by popular election, or perhaps by empowering the existing congress to take on the role. Arbitrary selection by the new leaders is not unknown. Constituent assemblies, whether continuations of existing congresses or not, frequently act in a larger capacity than their titles imply and perform the general legislative and other functions of regular congresses, frequently including the selection of the new president to serve under the new constitution.

Constitution by Decree. In a few cases, constitutions have been simply pronounced, or given, by the president or ruling juntas in the period following a *coup d'état.* Thus, the Brazilian constitution of 1937 was decreed by Getulio Vargas and thereafter put into force by his administration. Other cases involve such temporary measures as those in Cuba in 1952 (under Batista's sponsorship) and in Guatemala in 1954 (Castillo Armas), when sets of statutes were decreed to serve as fundamental law until constitutions could be drawn up.

The Suspension of Constitutional Provisions

One of the most remarkable aspects of Latin American constitutionalism is its sensitivity to crisis, usually due to the anxieties of the executive. The power of the president is frequently employed to deny the application of the constitution under certain conditions; occasionally the congress may be involved. The most widely used instrument in this maneuver is the state of siege (*estado de sitio*).[2] Nearly all Latin American constitutions provide for some form of this. Briefly, in certain emergency circumstances (threat of invasion, actual invasion, or serious internal crisis, for example), the executive, with the approval of congress if in session, can suspend rights guaranteed by the constitution. Provisions vary as to the extent and technique of state of siege. In the typical application, those rights associated with speech, press, assembly, and movement are denied, or perhaps restricted. This institution is attributable to European tradition, especially with regard to the protection of the medieval town; an even earlier ancestor is said to be the *senatus consultus ultimum,* an extraordinary action of the Roman Senate by which, among other things, it could appoint a dictator to serve with full powers for a limited period.

State of siege is frequently confused with martial law, although state of siege is basically a civil situation under ordinary policing methods and employing the ordinary courts. Not exactly comparable, either, is the suspension of the writ of *habeas corpus,* as provided in the constitution of the United States. The essence of all these is, to be sure, the same; the differences are evident in the techniques and breadth of application.

A typical state of siege imposes restriction of personal liberties for a certain period, usually thirty days. Often, however, there are renewals, so that the entire effect may spread over years. Some republics have been under state of siege for most of periods extending five years or more. It was reported in 1950 that El Salvador had spent almost all of the preceding 20 years under state of siege. During World War II, it was widely applied throughout Latin America as a whole.

Thus, the net effect of such a suspension of rights is to provide a considerable constitutional void within which the individual is closely controlled in the interest of the nation. In practice, this has often meant a distortion of the spirit of the constitutions, whereby an overzealous or overanxious executive attempts to restrict opposition to his administration; threats to the state may be real, imagined, or even staged.

The Role That Constitutions Play

Although many Latin American constitutions may not have been adequately tailored in the beginning and although there is much evidence to support the idea that these constitutions are still shakily attached to the culture, it should nevertheless be recorded that constitutions are not meaningless trappings.[3] They represent sincere goals and have, in many cases, now and in the past, provided limitations beyond which a regime dared not go. At the very least, many of the constitutions provide limitations beyond which there will be considerable reluctance to venture. Then, of course, it should be pointed out that a number of Latin American republics have experienced long periods of relatively "constitutional" behavior. The factor of potentiality is all too often overlooked in the assessment of political institutions, and nowhere is there a better example of this oversight than in the assessment of Latin American public affairs. It may be said that constitutions in Latin America, in those cases in which indifference to them has been apparent, are nevertheless the "conscience" of those in power. Who is to say that this is not itself an environmental influence at work?

Because of the extraordinary circumstances surrounding the creation of some Latin American constitutions, constitutions often take on the character of personal property. When a new regime takes power by *coup d'état*, it often feels that it cannot fly the banner of the old regime. It is a tarnished and perhaps reviled symbol that has been associated with an allegedly tyrannical regime. Therefore, a new one must be provided (even though often not substantially different in content) to herald and commemorate the new leadership. In Venezuela, at the time of this writing the constitution associated with the Pérez Jiménez regime is giving way to a new fundamental law to introduce the new era; similarly, in Argentina and Cuba, following the Perón and Batista administrations respectively, reactions have turned to reintroducing older constitutions that were the banners of revolt (the Argentine Constitution of 1853, which had been substantially amended under Perón's leadership, and the Cuban Constitution of 1940, which the rebels always publicly proclaimed had been destroyed by Batista).

In a very practical sense, therefore, constitutions often are announcements that the government is "under new management." Such constitutions are similar to stock prospectuses; they may or may not be accurate indications of future enrichment.

Another interesting view of some constitutions in Latin America is one that appeals to political theorists—that is, a new constitution more closely represents a timely social contract than an older constitution out of another era. This view is somewhat reminiscent of Jefferson's observation that constitutions should perhaps be renewed every generation. The hand of the living may thus constantly be free of the hand of the dead. In the framework of logic— if one accepts social dynamism as a constitutional reality —this appears to have a genuine ring. Unfortunately, this sort of justification for Latin American constitutional frequency appears to have the quality of rationalization rather than of fact. The fact is that frequency of constitutions is usually a product of unsettled political situations wherein the struggle is so recriminatory that the edifice of the outgoing regime must at the very least be repainted if not rebuilt.

Another view of Latin American constitutions is rooted in experience—the necessity to legalize. This has a dual application. In the first place, Latin Americans have a considerable fondness for legalism in the continental and formal sense, an inheritance of Roman law and jurisprudence. There is a ceremonial propriety suggested in this application. In the second place, a new regime frequently requires legal justification for its *de facto* status, a transformation from *de facto* to *de iure,* so to speak. A variation on this is observed in those cases in which a president wishes to continue in office and the existing constitution prevents re-election; a constituent assembly may conveniently provide a new constitution and at the same time elect the incumbent to be the "first" president under the new fundamental law, a practice commonly associated with the technique of *continuismo.*[4]

In summary, with reference to all Latin American republics, it may be said that constitutions are regarded as instrumentalities rather than as fountainheads. In all the republics there exists the possibility of substantial rearrangement under the leadership of strong executive action. Furthermore, even a constitution of long standing does not necessarily suggest preoccupation with "constitutionality" such as prevails in the United States.

The General Structure
of Latin American Governments

Although the life expectancy of a Latin American constitution may be short, nevertheless the general structure of Latin American governments presents strong continuity. There is substantial uniformity in the major structural elements of the republics. There are, of course, differences in the practice of government from one to another, but it may be said that these are all variations on a theme.

Presidential System. All the Latin American republics provide for presidential executives with the exception of Uruguay, where a conciliar or collegiate form of executive has recently been introduced. In the presidential system, the model of the United States shows clearly. The office of president appeared to be the product of circumstances in the United States that were also in evidence in Latin America during a similar independence movement, and, therefore, the leaders in most parts of Latin America thought of the presidential system as a precedent already established for antimonarchical reaction. It appeared to be an institutional solution to an old and discredited royalty. And, furthermore, even if one was still a monarchist, there was the practical problem of founding a great many royal houses. Only in Brazil was it possible to establish monarchy on a satisfactory basis, and even here, in a few decades, strong sentiment arose for republicanism, which finally was brought about in 1891.

Essentially, an adequate understanding of Latin American government centers on the activities of the presidents and presidential aspirants. This subject will be treated in some detail in later chapters.

Representative Basis. As republics, the Latin American states are founded on the principles of modern representation, with sovereignty placed in the people. Most Latin American constitutions, in the first article, described the basis of the system in terms of those principles—"representative," "democratic," "republican," or perhaps several such terms in combination.

Bicameralism flourishes in the national legislative bodies. Unicameral legislatures are found only in Costa Rica, Guatemala, Honduras, Panama, Paraguay, and El Salvador.

Separation of Powers. The separation-of-powers concept is espoused in much the same way as in the United States —that is, with compartmentalized branches, each presented with the opportunity, in theory at least, to check each of the others. However, many of the republics indicate a continental flair for some form of ministerial responsibility to the legislature and ministerial counterbalance to presidential action. Practice dictates that the president in fact effectively controls this intended check, as we shall see in later pages. The cabinet system has been effectively employed only in Chile during the years from 1891 to 1925. Some less effective cabinet systems have been sporadically active in Cuba and Peru, where, indeed, the office of Prime Minister has been employed.

Unitary Systems. Practically all Latin America has at some time been involved in an old problem of internal organization—the choice between unitary or federal organization. At the time of independence, federalism, along with other North American institutions, was very widely considered, to some extent, because of sentiment that equated North American federalism with successful republican experience. However, in some parts of Latin America, there were antecedents for federal organization. Eventually, Argentina, Brazil, Mexico, and Venezuela were organized on a federal basis. Colombia, Chile, Peru, and Central

America were among those that considered federalism with negative results.

In the Latin American area, therefore, unitary systems predominate. And, actually, even the federal systems tend in practice rather significantly toward centralization.

Civil Rights. Considerable attention is paid to civil rights in Latin American constitutions. Since most of these constitutions are the products of modern decades, they partake of the modern trend toward careful and full enumeration of individual and social rights. It is generally acknowledged that the pattern for this tendency may have originated with the Mexican Constitution of 1917, at least in matters that relate to the relationships springing from modern industrialism. Much earlier, during the movement to separate from the mother country, there was the heady inspiration of the American and French revolutions, both of which were rallies to the cause of the natural rights of man.

The Cuban Constitution of 1940 is a veritable monument to the accumulative impact of rights in modern constitutions. A total of 76 articles was devoted to this general concern, organized under the three titles of Fundamental Rights, Concerning Family and Culture, and Concerning Labor and Property. Most Latin American constitutions today go into some detail on all these matters, with increasing emphasis on the social function of property, capital, and economic activity.

It should be observed that these developments, although greatly emphasized in Latin America because of particular socio-economic problems, are receiving greater attention everywhere in the world of the mid-twentieth century. It is likely that if a national constitutional convention were to be held in the United States at this time, there would be a considerable temptation to enumerate at length the experience and aspirations as measured by modern life. Indeed, the tendencies toward greater length in general in the state constitutions may be an indication of this.

The General Impression. A reading of a typical Latin American constitution leaves the impression of a combination of North American structural design for policy-making and continental logic and symmetry in administrative organization and thoroughness of coverage. In the chapters that follow, we shall explore the institutions and techniques that provide the real flavor of Latin American government in practice.

CHAPTER THREE

The Electoral Process

The Latin American systems have committed themselves to the full machinery and spirit of democratic government. As the brief survey of constitutionalism has indicated, the new Latin American republics erected prefabricated institutions and then attempted to live in them. Democracy, of course, lends itself least readily to action based on lack of substance. It is more than faith and aspirations. In its most effective operation, it is clearly a societal situation in which substance preceded form. As Leo S. Rowe has pointed out, Latin American countries are engaged in a struggle "to bring their social organization into closer harmony with their political institutions." [1]

In surveying the electoral process, we shall encounter both the promise and the unreality of effective democratic government in parts of Latin America.

35

Political Awareness

The raw material of which effective representative government is made is a society presented with the awareness of the political activity and the freedom to act in accordance with information freely acquired. It is not necessary that all members of the society be constantly engaged in this activity; it is only necessary that they be free to engage in it. There is very wide agreement that a healthy awareness and freedom of political action are to a considerable degree dependent on such socio-economic factors as literacy, education, satisfaction of physical needs to some moderate level, and the possibility of fulfillment of social aspirations.[2]

An official publication of the United Nations describes the peasants of underdeveloped areas as the "forgotten men" of the twentieth century.[3] Most of Latin America falls into the classification of "underdeveloped," if by this we mean the lack of sufficient exploitation of resources to maintain an adequate standard of living. Most of Latin America is a rural economy and, as already noted, the land-tenure systems have not favored the development of small holdings sufficient to keep a family supplied with the necessities of life. This is the pattern in all parts of Latin America except parts of Costa Rica, Haiti, El Salvador, and Mexico.

The annual per capita income of all of Latin America falls into the lowest categories. In only seven of the republics does the income rise above $250 per year.

Although everywhere improving to some extent, the conditions affecting health are such as to produce comparatively low life expectancies. Unsanitary surroundings, diet deficiencies, and the lack of medical facilities lay large parts of the populations open to tuberculosis, malaria, intestinal infections, and skin diseases. In 1954, it was reported that in Paraguay there were 412 physicians, of whom 331 were located in the capital city. Substandard dwellings house most Latin American families, especially in rural areas and in low-income urban districts.

One of the most marked social characteristics of Latin American life is the presence of high degrees of illiteracy. Only a few of the republics can boast of literacy percentages that exceed 75% (Argentina, Chile, Costa Rica, Cuba, and Uruguay); at least seven of the republics fall below 50%. All the republics provide for compulsory education for an average of six years, but school attendance rarely meets expectations based on the number of children eligible to attend.

The socio-economic factors thus far mentioned have been aggravated by the fact that Latin America is rapidly increasing in population; indeed, it has been reported that this rate of increase is greater than that in any other part of the world. To some unknown extent, of course, this is a measure of improvement in the conditions that have contributed to high infant-mortality rates in the past.

If one were to summarize the effects of these socio-economic factors upon political awareness, one would be compelled to note that political activity in such circumstances will very likely be confined to the few educated and generally privileged citizens. Furthermore, there will be a great likelihood that "revolution," which makes a bid for change in the socio-economic situation (whether possible of fulfillment or not), will be very appealing to the mass of underprivileged. Finally, with respect to the matter of comparative historical experiences, Latin American political life lacks the solidity and orderliness that a middle class has been able to implant in the soils of other countries that moved into industrialism at an earlier time.[4] The Latin American republics vaulted into a world not of their making—the world of industrial nations with mighty resources including human skills, already in motion for a long time, and already in command of trade on a global scale. Still, with a situation more favorable to playing this game, Latin America might have found a more secure place in it before now. Only now, at mid-twentieth century, are the beginnings of some place in this system coming into evidence.

Political Parties

The Latin American scene offers a rich variety of political parties.[5] Since the colonial period was not a climate favorable to the creation of parties, the political histories of Latin America with respect to such organized political action begin with the struggles for the organization of the republics. In the early years of these struggles, there developed two types of partisan division. One natural division was of the ageless conservative-liberal character, the conservative forces representing in general the aspirations of the new creole elite allied with traditional Church and propertied interests and, opposed to them, those groups looking to secular control of Church and the uplifting of lower social orders. Another type of division, sometimes coinciding with the first, was federal-unitarian in nature. The lines were never clearly drawn, of course, and rising above all of it was the ultimate determinant in the person of the *caudillo*. In many cases, the personal struggle between *caudillos* was all that could be pretended as political action.

At the close of the nineteenth century, in a number of the republics in which industrialism had made some inroads, parties were formed along lines then in vogue in Europe, particularly socialist parties. Since that time, there has been a constant reflection in Latin America of organized political groups contending in the European arena.

Legal Definitions. A typical Latin American republic regulates the political party system in quite the manner now fashionable in most modern systems. In Latin America there tends to be a rather greater display of favoritism toward the "government party," which can be very easily accomplished through the ordinary channels of law-making and administrative interpretations. Parties are given legal definition in the usual way—that is, by formal registration by petition. In some cases, the petition requirement is severe, as in Mexico where the prospective party must produce a registration of 75,000 voters with at least 2,500 registrants in each of at least two-thirds of the states. During the Perón regime in Argentina, new parties could not be recognized until the end of a three-year period, during which time the application was passed upon by electoral courts; old parties had to be passed upon by the electoral courts also, although they were not subject to the waiting period. Much depends, always, upon the whim and tolerance of the existing government.

Certain kinds of parties may be outlawed altogether. They include Communists (in practically all the republics), parties that "endanger social peace" (in Perón's Argentina), such specific parties as the *Apristas* (until recently in Peru), and parties that receive assistance from abroad (in several republics).

Nomenclature. An inspection of the titles of the parties is of some interest in itself. Very common are titles that feature such terms as "revolutionary," "popular," "socialist," and "radical." Here are party titles that have been in use in Bolivia in recent years: Socialist Republicans, Genuine Republicans, Socialists, Leftist Revolutionary, Liberals; in Costa Rica: Republican, Popular Vanguard, National Union, Social Democrat, National Brotherhood, Liberal, Civic Progressive, and National Liberation, among others.

A very common political party tactic is the coalition organized into "movements," "unions," "fronts," or "alliances." Thus, a few years ago, in Peru, one found such a combination in the National Democratic Front and in Guatemala, the National Anti-Communist Front, Democratic Electoral Front, and the National Democratic Front. These coalitions are ordinarily for purposes of electing presidents, and very frequently they do not hold together after the election has been decided.

Finally, it should be noted that throughout Latin America it is common to use a popularized name for the party in which the party leader is featured: *Vargistas, Peronistas, Ibañistas, Herreristas.* Indeed, the term *Peronista* was in the official title of the party as well, an unusual recognition of *personalismo* in party nomenclature.

Personalities and Issues. On the whole, political parties in Latin America are not founded as strongly on issues as they are on personalities. *Personalismo* accounts for the great majority of parties in all but a few republics. Many parties rise and fall at election time, temporary vehicles for the aspirations of the leader of the group—a fact reflected in the tendency to refer to the party by its popular personalized title. To some extent, an opposition party may keep its identity under a defeated leader, but usually, at the next election a very thorough reorganization of loyalty will be required to keep it alive. Between elections it will rarely be of any effect.

The political parties tend to fall into four types: (1) parties that are purely personal and usually ephemeral in effect; (2) parties that are purely personal but enjoy a considerable opportunity to exercise power; (3) parties that are associated with some deeply intrenched tradition or decisive historical event (such as revolution) and form reservoirs for the selection of a succession of leaders; (4) parties that are securely attached to such issues as socio-economic advancement or traditional conservativism. Examples of the first type have existed in very great numbers and tend to flourish in most of the republics at election time, although many of them, in the face of electoral reality, disappear into "fronts" that will plump for a particular candidate. A very striking example of the second type was the approximately ten-year administration of Argentina under the *Peronistas.*[6] This party was a most extraordinary exhibition of *personalismo* raised to the heights of a cult (see Chapter 6). The best example of the third type is the Institutional Revolutionary Party (PRI) of Mexico (see following paragraphs); another in this category would be the Cuban Revolutionary Party. In the fourth type would fall the socialist and communist parties and, to some lesser extent, parties such as the *Apristas* in Peru, Democratic Action in Venezuela, and the National Revolutionary Movement in Bolivia. Conservative parties are to be found in a number of republics under various titles; they are perhaps most prominent at the moment in Chile, Colombia, Ecuador, Peru, and Venezuela.

Variations in Systems. The only realistic way to view the Latin American parties is to view them against the background of their own national systems. In these systems we find variety—multi-party, two-party, and one-party systems.

Over recent decades, about half the republics have maintained multi-party systems in which parties are to be found spanning the spectrum from an occasional fascist or extreme rightist group through conservatives, moderates of right through left center, to socialist and communist parties. The best and most constant example of this scheme is Chile, which has during modern decades offered the full spectacle of ideological spread from right to left.[7] It is the common procedure in Chilean presidential elections to form at least three groups of right, center, and left for the massive assault upon the presidency, each group, however, consisting of many parties who will reassert their independence in the Congress. Within the past decade the following parties have been active in Chilean politics, the enumeration running from right to left, ideologically speaking· Conservative, Traditional Conservative, Social Christian Conservative, Liberal, Independent, Agrarian, Progressive Liberal, National Falangist, Radical, Democrat, Socialist, Popular Socialist, and Communist. In Brazil, Cuba, and Guatemala, a similar spread has occasionally been found.

In a number of the republics, one observes two-party

systems, although they present some variety. The purest example is to be found in Colombia, where for generations the Liberals and the Conservatives have engaged in political struggle, a struggle that became civil war from 1948 through 1954. This is a two-party system like that of the United States in one respect—each party contains within it a rather wide spread of ideological content, but presents a difference in degree on the average. The Conservative-Liberal struggle in Colombia has often appeared to have the nature of a social feud rather than ordinary political differences. Uruguay has in some respects the character of a two-party system in the perennial struggle between the *Colorados* and *Blancos;*[8] it must be noted, by way of qualification, that each of the parties has, in effect, factions (*sublemas*), each with separate standing in the law and each running separate candidates for congressional posts. In Argentina during the Perón years, there was a two-party system, in which a very harassed Radical Party attempted to oppose the *Peronistas.* Honduras, Nicaragua, and El Salvador have employed what amount to two-party systems.

There are three prominent one-party systems, although each calls for a separate approach because of the very different circumstances: in the Dominican Republic, Mexico, and Paraguay. In general, it may be said that the one-party systems in the Dominican Republic and in Paraguay have been the result of intimidation on the part of the governing party, in the Dominican Republic the Dominican Party and in Paraguay the *Colorados.*

In Mexico, one finds an extraordinary party in the Institutional Revolutionary Party (PRI).[9] Although there is some opposition in elections, it has been so ineffectual as to place such opposition parties in the class with minor parties in the United States. This party is the institutional inheritance of the Mexican Revolution; at first, it rode successfully as the active agent of the Revolution and then gradually managed to stand somewhat independent of the active revolutionary role and to continue its domination by a combination of momentum generated by early success and willingness to accommodate itself to the times. It has managed this transition so successfully that it maintains within itself the role of opposition as well as leadership, somewhat as the Democratic party does in some southern states in the United States. It has not hesitated to use the overpowering weight of government in its own behalf, but at the same time it has kept its ears well attuned to the public. It has chosen presidents who have symbolized the times—from the revolutionary Calles, to the active leftist Cárdenas, to transitional Camacho, to the businessman-lawyer Aleman, to the bureaucrat Ruiz Cortines, and finally to the labor-management mediator López Mateos. Its flexibility is well demonstrated by the fact that Cárdenas is still a power in the party. These successive changes in the party leadership mirror the progress of the Mexican state from raw revolutionary leadership to the first stages of a middle-class-dominated industrial state.

Other Organized Interests

As in every modern nation, there are organized interests in Latin America that fall outside the particular form of the political party. The pressure group, as it is known in the United States, exists to a much lesser extent in Latin America and the techniques employed differ. The main procedural difference lies in the fact that a group's approach in a typical Latin American government is to the president rather than to the legislative branch, because the legislature is ordinarily subsidiary to executive domination. More important than the "trade association" or farm organizations are the organizations that can take a direct approach by virtue of a broader appeal to some traditional group in the society.

The Church.[10] The prominence of the Roman Catholic Church in Latin American life includes, in most of the republics, considerable political influence. There is, of course, difference in degree among the republics. In general, it should be noted that although substantial anti-clericalism may be found in a few republics (such as Mexico), the Church has not lost great numbers of adherents. In Mexico, indeed, in the last decade or more, the Church has come more openly into prominence.

Traditionally the Church—or at least the higher members of the hierarchy—has stood with conservative interests. It has, of course, stood by the papal encyclicals of the twentieth century, which have in general pleaded for social justice, but in its concern for considerable traditionalism, it has often stood with orderly regimes, even if they have bristled with force and defiance of progress. Very deeply buried in the Church's attitude is a distrust of secular instruments for societal improvement. Occasionally, however, the lower orders of the hierarchy engage in essentially political movements of liberal intent, as in Costa Rica, where Padre Nuñez actively organized such a movement. The classic case of Father Hidalgo in the early days of the Mexican Revolution is well known.

The Church may employ its strength by direct appeals that can have decidedly significant effect on the political *status quo.* It was the entrance of the Church into the fray in Argentina that pushed a declining Perón into a position of desperation from which he could not recover. For a time before his last year, Perón had openly opposed the Church on issues that were bound to be irreconcilable, such as divorce legislation.

Labor.[11] Organized labor is prominent in much of Latin America, particularly in mining and industrial areas. Some activity, to be sure, is to be found in agricultural areas, as, for example, in Bolivia and Mexico. Strikes have occurred frequently in Argentina, Brazil, and Chile.

The distinctive feature of labor-union activity in Latin America is the inevitably high degree of direct engagement of the government. When a labor-management dispute breaks out in Latin America, the government may in

fact be the employer, because much of industry is nationalized, particularly in transportation and communication. If the government is not itself the employer, it is
ordinarily granted a role of direct interest by the constitutions and the laws. A typical Latin American constitution
now contains voluminous material on labor affairs, inevitably involving the direct regulatory activity of government agencies. In addition to this administrative relationship, the tendency of government to "intervene" in much
of economic life as incidental to the peace and good order
of the state is very common.

In view of these matters, labor unions in Latin America
are very anxious to gain strength and privilege within
government. They have managed to find a considerable
voice in the PRI in Mexico. In Bolivia, they are very
securely engaged in the government under the National
Revolutionary Movement. Whether in or out of influence,
the unions in Chile have provided almost constant prodding
and have brought much intervention on the part of the
government.

The pressing forward of organized labor in Latin
America has given rise to one of the more spectacular developments in recent decades—riding militant labor union-
ism into political power. The Perón regime was the most
thoroughly organized example, although the National
Revolutionary Movement in Bolivia, Vargas' Labor Party
in Brazil, and, to some extent, the *Ibañistas* in Chile
attempted the same approach in principle.

The "Oligarchs." A very common term in the recriminatory
literature of Latin American politics is "oligarch," applied
to the privileged land-holding class and, to a lesser extent
in a few republics, to the "big businessman." For many
decades in the nineteenth and twentieth centuries, a great
part of Latin America was controlled by this group, either
directly in some type of conservative party or behind the
scenes through economic and social pressure. Their activities were particularly effective in Argentina, Chile, Ecuador,

Peru, and Venezuela. The influence of the "oligarchs" has declined everywhere, although it is not out of the picture by any means.

The influence of such interests is not ordinarily achieved by such organized groups as the Chamber of Commerce or the National Association of Manufacturers in the United States. Rather, they have exercised their strength in a more personal and direct fashion.

Students. Latin American students take an active part in political life. As a comparatively small number of intellectuals, who will soon probably take up leading posts in professional life, they are socially more privileged and generally more honored in these republics than, for example, in the United States. They are usually organized into federations, which may be legally recognized bodies, defined and regulated by law. Thus, the internal political life of the student federation may be a prelude of conflict to come in the national arena. One of the most active federations is in the University of Havana in Cuba.

Student life in a typical Latin American university (most of which are national universities) is like that of the old European tradition in which the students involve themselves substantially in university administrative affairs. In addition, they take a very intense interest in national and international politics.

It is quite common for university students to stage demonstrations, strikes, and parades, during which a direct challenge to government policy is presented. Frequently, violence results. Occasionally, a student strike will be the signal for a general demonstration in which shopkeepers and workers may join. On the other hand, student sympathy with the government can sometimes be so stirred up in its patriotic sensitivity as to engage the opposition by direct means.

In many of the smaller republics, a student demonstration can bring about immediate attention to the grievance. In Guatemala, in 1950, the students struck in an action against the Minister of Interior; the resignation of that official followed. In Panama, in 1946, a student strike brought about an immediate conference with the President of the republic. The actions of an enraged student body following the coup staged by Batista in Cuba in 1952 prefaced a continuing opposition culminating in the Castro revolution of 1959.

The Military Forces. A description of the very significant role of the military in politics, including frequent and direct intervention in national affairs, will be developed in later pages (see especially Chapter 4).

Women in Politics. Women have come into the electoral picture in Latin America with considerable force in the years following World War II. They may now participate in the electoral process and hold office in most of the republics. In only a few instances, however, have they organized in any distinctive way. The most outstanding version, perhaps without an equal anywhere, was the feminine branch of the *Peronistas,* under the direction of the unparalleled Eva Perón in Argentina. In Chile and Mexico, much less pretentious women's organizations have been organized. A number of women have held political posts in a number of the republics.

Elections

The ultimate mechanical feature of democratic or quasi-democratic systems is the casting of ballots for the officials who will make and administer policy. As already indicated, the Latin American systems, however much one may quarrel with the actual degree of real democracy in some republics, employ the machinery that modern representative systems have come to use for this central act of accountability.[12]

Voting Qualifications. Nearly all the republics have now provided for universal adult suffrage, with perhaps occasional limitations on women's suffrage. Considerable variety exists among the republics on specific qualifications, as might be expected among 20 separate nations. Generally speaking, men and women may vote, either at 18 or 21. Literacy tests are common, although they are not always thoroughly enforced. Occasionally, a distinction is made on the basis of marital status, perhaps allowing married males to vote at 18 rather than 21, for example.

Registration and Credentials. Registration of voters is usually carried out painstakingly in accordance with a system prescribed by national legislation. The typical system is a hierarchy of boards (*juntas, consejos,* etc.), pyramiding into a national board, which perhaps oversees a national director whose job it is to co-ordinate the system. The whole process—and indeed more broadly the whole electoral process—is the responsibility of the Minister of the Interior (in Mexico, Minister of Government).

The evidence of registration is a voter's card, called by various names—*libreta, credencial,* or *boleta.* Invariably this card must be presented at election time, and it is usually stamped by an election official with some indication that the person has voted. The voter's card may contain considerable information, with perhaps fingerprints and a photograph. Much fraud has been perpetrated in connection with voters' credentials; for example, many of them may be collected before an election under some pretext or other in order to prevent certain opposition groups from voting. And, on the other hand, in some more authoritarian systems, particularly in the past, the presentation of one's card showing evidence of having voted the "right way" would be necessary to receive ordinary courtesies and service from governmental agencies.

Nominations. In Latin America, there is no process similar to the direct primary as employed in the United States. The major nominating procedure concerns presidential candidates and takes place in party conventions as in the

United States. Typically, after the presidential nomination, party lists for congress are built up, determined by the party leadership in harmony with the presidential race. There may be involved elaborate alliances of parties, combining on a presidential candidate, but offering separate lists for congressional posts. From this level down to local elections (and including congressional races in off years), the procedure is much the same—essentially, determination of candidates by the party leadership. The formality of filing one's name for candidacy, backed by a certain number of petitioners, is common.

In countries where the government party's nominee for president is certain to win, there is likely to be a constant charge of *imposición* leveled at the government (as is the unvarying lament of opposition candidates in Mexican elections). The extreme form is called *candidato único;* the government candidate may indeed be the "only candidate" in the race. This situation may occur either by virtue of ruling the opposition candidates off the ballot (as in Peru in 1950, when Odría's opponent was so treated) or by choice of the opposition to abstain from the election (common in Colombia from 1948 through 1954, when the Liberals refused to take part).

Elections. Electoral laws in Latin America change frequently, and it is difficult, therefore, to keep abreast of the precise machinery of voting in all republics. The chief administrator of the electoral process invariably is the Minister of Interior—even in federal systems—although the canvassing and handling of disputes are usually handled by boards or tribunals (*cortes, jurados,* etc.), which are usually appointed by the president, sometimes from lists supplied from the parties. Frequently, they are strongly disposed to judge in favor of the government party.

Typically, voting is done throughout a single day— usually Sunday—with the polling places open from an early hour to early evening. There are the usual officials in charge —local electoral councils (*consejos*) or some similar organization (*comité* or *directorio*). These usually consist of from three to five members for each polling place; the polling is done at a level not unlike precincts in the United States (*circuito, barrio, distrito*). Until very recently, at least, voting was still done in a few places in full view, thus allowing a certain amount of intimidation. The typical method is, however, secret. Presentation of the voter's card is required, and it is usually stamped or otherwise marked to prevent reuse. In addition to this precaution, a few republics still require that a finger or thumb be dipped in indelible ink. The procedure for marking ballots varies; in many cases, marking is not necessary since one simply selects the party list of his preference and discards the others. Ballots are often distinctively colored to indicate the various parties; this is sometimes a means of detecting how a voter is voting.

The counting of ballots is the stage that often arouses great controversy. Although the count is made by apparently multi-party boards, the government party is usually able to dominate the proceedings. One of the most startling cases of government domination occurred in Venezuela in 1952, when, in an election thought "safe" for Pérez Jiménez, the ballots were apparently going against the government; accordingly, the process was halted, and later Pérez Jiménez was declared "elected."

Boycotted Elections. One of the most common electoral feature of Latin America is the abstention from participation by an opposition party as a dramatic way of indicating the futility of opposing the government. The strategy is to make the victory of the government as hollow as possible and thereby give substance to later charges that the government has only a half-hearted mandate. The boycott may start as early as the nomination process or may be adopted later, even after the ballots have been printed. If the offended party has already chosen a candidate for president, for example, and the decision is made to boycott the coming election, the presidential candidate will make a dramatic appeal to the supporters of his candidacy to stay away from the polls. This was the case in Cuba in 1954, when Grau Martín withdrew from the race against Batista, intimating that the election was going to be rigged. The Liberals in Colombia abstained during a long period of civil disturbance from 1948 to 1954.

Post-electoral Activity. A typical Latin American election may extend beyond the announcement of the results, in effect. Frequently, a defeated candidate for the presidency, in particular, is unwilling to accept the results and will indicate that "fraud" and "intimidation" accompanied the electoral process. Occasionally disappointed followers rally to this call and violence results.

There is more involved here than the charge of fraudulent handling of electoral machinery. The excessive personalism of Latin American politics does not subside easily; the loser feels a personal affront at the results; and even if he can swallow this, frequently his followers cannot. For in a presidential election a very great deal is at stake for the followers of a candidate. In a typical Latin American republic, bureaucratic positions are very eagerly sought as a means of livelihood or at least as a necessary supplement to one's professional income, which may be very slight.

Finally, in the histories of some of the republics, it is to be noted that appeal to force has indeed been the only real recourse for upsetting the government party, which is disposed to use any means to stay in office. Revolution itself may in such circumstances appear to be a sort of electoral technique.

Free Elections

Although no doubt exists as to the very substantial impact of the "ins" on the electoral process in nearly all the republics, it should be observed that free elections have frequently been held and that these are increasing in number in our time. It is more difficult to insure free campaigning, because the zeal of the government party usually guarantees the denial of at least some services to the opposition—in the matter of posters, radio and television, transportation, and perhaps even ordinary courtesies in hotels. The trend is everywhere in the direction of toning down this impact of the government although it may be some time yet before substantial improvement is evident in some areas.

CHAPTER FOUR

Revolution, Violence,

Political Morality

The most widely observed—and possibly the least under-stood—characteristic of Latin American politics is the frequent use of force. The United States seems to be particularly aware of this manifestation, although judg-ments are often made by standards different from those applicable in Latin America. Still, the fact remains that the observation is correct. Not long ago a president of Ecuador, Eduardo Galo Plaza Lasso, is reported to have remarked about the quelling of an attempt to unseat the government: "I am witnessing a demonstration of the national sport." [1] Whatever exaggeration or humor he may have intended, his comment nevertheless indicates the presence of a very real factor of considerable significance in the political process. Some investigation of this element of force and some excursion into political morality appear fitting at this time in order to assess properly the practical instruments of Latin American politics. It is undeniable that the socio-economic background already discussed is fundamental to this whole problem.

Revolution and Its Meanings

One of the first considerations is the choice of words to describe adequately what takes place. The word most widely used is "revolution." But it is so liberally applied that it includes a large number of situations not ordinarily included within the range of definitions. Latin Americans themselves—and particularly the leaders of a movement—are likely to use this word rather loosely. It is used to refer to mere *coups;* it is used to refer to a long-range revolutionary process; and, finally, it may refer to Revolution. Most of the "revolutions" are of the first type and will be discussed later. With respect to the second type, Latin America, in company with much of the world, has been participating to some degree in such long-range processes as an industrial revolution; it is not necessary to explore here such an obvious and ubiquitous process.

Revolution—with a capital R—has been extremely rare. In this type, we are concerned with the dramatic surges and upheavals that have shaken the roots of systems and brought drastic changes in the societies involved. In such a category we are accustomed to speak of the French Revolution or the Bolshevik Revolution. It may be proper to speak of the war for independence from Spain, waged by the Latin American colonies, as being of this type. In the life of the Latin American republics, however, only one revolution appears to be generally recognized as such—the Mexican Revolution of 1910 and following years. In some other cases, one occasionally hears similar sentiments—regarding, for example, the National Revolutionary Movement in Bolivia. At the moment of writing, there is considerable sentiment for the inclusion in this exclusive company of the successful Castro movement in Cuba and the return of the Democratic Action in Venezuela, but actually it is too early to say.

The word "revolution" in most of the major Western nations suggests horror, chaos, and irrationality. The fact is, of course, that each of these nations had revolutionary experiences at earlier times in their histories. Not so long ago the very life of the Western world seemed to be expressed in the vigorous language of revolution. Thomas Jefferson wrote of it as if it were a normal social impulse, necessary to clear the air periodically. Many modern Latin American "revolutionary" leaders have thought of their movements as equally necessary, glorious, and praiseworthy. The fact that few will deserve the term "revolution" does not lessen the zeal nor render the movement inglorious in the eyes of the zealous. Young countries with unfulfilled social, economic, and nationalistic goals will undoubtedly always have a revolution—at the very least, in blueprint. Each new movement having some substantial momentum from "the unfulfilled" will very likely be considered a revolution; if it turns to disillusionment, then the next time will be the revolution. The great number of Latin American political parties with "revolution" in their titles attest to this expectation.

What happens to Latin American "revolutions"? Some are not genuinely inspired and are mere *coups*, by which power shifts from one part of the governing class to another (see section below on *coup d'état*); some are thoroughly squashed before they gain sufficient momentum; and some, facing the realities of governing or the temptations of power, become ordinary political parties.

The Military Role

Anyone with only a nodding acquaintaince with Latin American public affairs realizes the important role played by the military organizations in many of the republics.[2] Military prowess and military professionalism have always ranked high in the Iberian culture, as is evidenced by the part they played on the peninsula and in colonial times. So high did the military stand at the time of independence that the Argentine statesman Alberdi was compelled to describe military glory as "the supreme object of ambition." [3] The very difficult organizational years were in large part characterized by the clash of military *caudillos;* the tradition was thus kept strong at a very critical and formative period in the lives of the republics.

In young, underdeveloped countries, the military impact on politics has always been marked. In the mid-twentieth century, this activity is apparent in the Middle East and the Far East.[4] Struggles quite like those of the *caudillos* in Latin America are evident in the Indo-Chinese area. For several decades, the military have been in the vanguard of movements in such countries as Syria, Turkey, and Egypt.

Organization. The military forces in a typical Latin American republic are not large by the standards of major nations. In countries like Bolivia, Ecuador, and Paraguay, the army may total less than 10,000 men and officers, which would be a force approximately the size of one division in the organization of a major military power. In Nicaragua, an army of 3,000 is apparently all that is thought necessary in the existing situation. One republic, Costa Rica, prides itself on maintaining a larger number of teachers than military troops and, at the present time, apparently has no standing army other than a national police force. On the other hand, in the larger republics of Argentina, Brazil, and Mexico, military forces (including naval and air branches) well in excess of 50,000 are employed. The distribution of forces also admits of considerable variation. One finds that in Mexico there is a widespread system of military regions, divided into 33 military zones. On the other hand, it is reported that the major part of the Paraguayan forces is made up of one cavalry division maintained in the vicinity of the capital.

Military budgets have often constituted a greater part of the total governmental expenditures than appear warranted. Partly accountable for this fact is undoubtedly that the ratio of commissioned officers to the total force has been traditionally large. Also partly accountable is the fact that frequently the budget for ordinary police forces is included in the total military outlay. Very handsome pension arrangements must be considered, too, especially for generals who have been kept on the payrolls although actually in exile. A number of the republics have recently improved the officer-enlisted men ratio; Mexico, for example, under a streamlining edict by President Camacho in 1945, managed to lower the ratio from one in 58 to one in 85, largely by eliminating generals without real commands.

Many commissioned officers receive part of their training abroad. Before World War II, it was not uncommon for many to study in Germany and Italy; others studied in England, France, and the United States. With the emphasis on hemispheric unity after World War II, more are studying in the United States than ever before; and United States military assistance programs have also been set up in Latin American countries.

Reservoir of Ambitions. Obviously, the military ranks, particularly among commissioned officers, offer considerable opportunity—socially and politically. Here is the springboard for many a prominent public figure in Latin American societies. The military service is an excellent medium for the expression of *personalismo* in all its forms, even ultimately its most powerful—the presidency. The smartly uniformed officer with leadership qualities can make himself widely known in public life. Indeed, it may be possible for him to do so while still only a captain or a major. Perón was a greatly admired sportsman when he was only a captain. Significant *coups* have been engineered on many occasions by younger officers. Witness the "majors' revolution" in El Salvador, led by Major Osorio a few years ago, or the young captains and majors in the persons of Pérez Jiménez and his clique in Venezuela in 1948. Batista, indeed, first came to power at the head of a successful sergeants' *coup* in Cuba in 1933. Among the younger officers, ambitions run high, and the sparring apparently begins at an early stage in some of their careers. This stirring among the younger officers can be accounted for in a number of ways. In the first place, the higher ranking officers often seem content with their lot at the top of the ranks, socially and probably financially; secondly, the younger officers are of course directly in command of the troops and represent the vital, direct force; lastly, among the younger officers, one is more likely to discover the more passionate preoccupation with ideals, patriotism, and socio-economic conditions.

Guardians of the National Spirit. In Latin America, the frequency and facility with which professional militarism can move into active political life is marked. The training of military officers stresses patriotism and national honor, of course, and military officers in all countries may well think that they are keeping aloft these ideals in the face of indifference elsewhere in the society. In Latin America, the nature of politics heightens these sentiments. Military officers—however mistaken they may sometimes be—frequently conclude that they must move forward into politics to keep up the moral and spiritual tone. Furthermore, much raw ambition may be masked by lip service to these ideals.

In short, military officers often find themselves carrying out a social mission. Always, it will be justified in the most glowing terms relating to the highest of ideals. Occasionally, the circumstances appear to offer reasonable justification. For example, whatever may have been the unfortunate later results in Colombia, General Rojas Pinilla stepped into public life in the midst of a civil war that, at the time, appeared irresolvable by other means (in the summer of 1953, after nearly six years of internal struggle). On many occasions—and perhaps the majority in which the military intervenes—intervention seems unwarranted and sometimes appears to be a bald seizure of power. But on all such occasions, the announcements are the same: the national honor, order, and safety require strong methods. Very frequently there is the suggestion that the new leaders are indeed neutral in the political sense. Thus General Odría, after the 1948 *coup* in Peru, stated that he was simply a "nationalist" interested in "social justice." [5] General Rojas Pinilla of Colombia stated that it "would be sacrilegious for me to exchange the national flag for one of a political party." [6]

The Wall of Isolation. With the military standing ready to carry out a selective function, it can be appreciated that the presidents of Latin American republics are extremely sensitive to any untoward movements from the barracks. One active participant, President Prío Socarrás of Cuba, in 1949, found a very picturesque phrase for this uneasiness. Having been informed that some suspicious rumblings were being heard from the army, he immediately investigated (at one o'clock in the morning) and removed the chief of staff, who, the President said, had erected a "wall of isolation" between him and the army.[7] The "wall of isolation" is invariably a sign that speed is essential. The president must personally test his system of loyalty and get in direct contact with the military leaders. How far has the matter gone? Has a sufficient number of pivotal officers been drawn into another loyalty system?

One frequently finds the term "praetorianism" used to describe this situation. In many situations the term is quite accurately applied. Like the Roman emperor, dependent on the praetorian guard, the Latin American president in many of the republics must be quick to maintain the support of the armed forces. The fact that the president is himself commander-in-chief of the armed forces is not necessarily a factor in the matter.

Because many Latin American presidents have come out of the military service and many have moved directly from active military intervention into politics, an additional element of skill and sensitivity, born of experience, enters the affair. "Leaks" of secret plots are quite common, and, to a certain extent, they measure the in-service affiliation that the president has been able to maintain. Frequently the president remains on the active promotion list; and, if he enters the presidency at the rank of colonel, he will periodically receive promotions until he holds, say, the permanent rank of general. In many cases, it is not proper to advance too rapidly. It must be kept in mind that the president may not be, to his former brother officers, quite the exalted figure that his present status suggests.

One of the institutional factors in the military important to in-service loyalty is the secret military society. Within the secrecy and ritual of such a group may be born a strong nucleus with considerable implication for the existing political situation. In Argentina, for example, the GOU (Group of United Officers) proved to be a spring-board for the ambitious Perón; and, apparently even before the arrival of Perón at the heights, it had set forth a program for the advancement of Argentine nationalism and prestige.

The Coup d'État

As pointed out earlier, most political moves born of force in Latin America are, properly speaking, *coups d'état* and not revolutions. That is to say, the most common move of force is a shift of power from one group to another without the substantial change characteristically suggested by revolution. There will be no appreciable change in philosophy, structure, or even socio-economic programs. To the mass of people in many of the republics, these are power games, played at the top without any noticeable change as far as their lot and aspirations are concerned.

As a technique for the seizure of power, a *coup d'état* involves merely the strategic placement of force in those vital places controlling the functions and particularly the communications network of government. Occasionally, the president is confronted and a resignation wrung from him. If the president has had adequate warning, he may already have sought a place of refuge or left the country.

This move is thought preferable, since it will allow the displaced executive to point out that he is still technically the president of the republic. Very often the whole affair passes quickly without any show of violence; the populace is simply informed of the change, and the matter ends. Very often a *coup* fails, thus bringing swift justice to the leaders. The president may have had the greater force still loyal to him. Or, occasionally, he may by frantic appeals and fence-mending renew loyalties and turn the disaster against some of his enemies. If there is a serious military problem—for example, an invasion by a well-supplied and disciplined army of "irregulars"—the president may be asked by loyal officers to face the realities and turn over the government to a group that can seek better terms. Such appeared to be the case when President Arbenz faced a very difficult situation as Castillo Armas swept into Guatemala, intent upon unseating the government; the last stages of resistance were directed by a junta while Arbenz absented himself from the scene. In effect, a *coup* of expediency was instituted.

A great number of unsuccessful *coups* are reported each year in Latin America. It is not always clear if in fact a *coup* was underway. It is undoubtedly, in an overanxious moment, easy to sense danger when it is not actually present. And one need not have too much imagination to appreciate that it might seem convenient to put an enemy into prison before any damage can be done. But the fact remains that many of these "nipped" *coups* are genuinely active movements, poised to take power or perhaps already involved in the attempt. A *coup* met head on can, of course, develop considerable violence, bloodshed, and subsequently severe punishments.

In the ten-year period from 1945 through 1954, reliable sources reported 70 or more *coups* throughout Latin America. Of these, 18 were successful, although in some cases for only a very short time before countermoves succeeded. Attempted *coups* were reported in every republic except the Dominican Republic and Mexico (and

Mexico experienced some local disturbances). In four of the republics there were over five such events each—Bolivia, Ecuador, Paraguay, and Venezuela. Successful *coups* were staged in Bolivia, Costa Rica, Colombia, Cuba, Ecuador, Guatemala, Nicaragua, Paraguay, Peru, El Salvador, and Venezuela, in some cases more than once. The circumstances differed widely, of course, although in terms of technique they were the same. In Paraguay, *coups* have usually been carried out as a sort of factionalism within the ruling clique; in Peru and Venezuela, military guardianship was applied to put down an apparently popular party; in Colombia, the military intervened for the first time in one hundred years; and in El Salvador, young officers set out to reform an old quasi-feudal order. It might be said that within the range of differences, varying degrees of justification could be found; still, the determinant was force and the technique, the *coup d'état*.

Invariably, following a *coup,* a provisional government is set up in the form of a junta. The typical junta consists of from three to seven members, usually dominated by military leaders. The junta presides until a return to constitutional government can be accomplished through elections. This may take several years; and, during much of this time, the junta may rule by decree. Typically, a constitutional convention is called to bring forth a constitution and perhaps also to serve as the congress. In the meantime, the provisional government is said to have *de facto* status; occasionally this status will be pronounced by the supreme court. The present policy of the United States extends recognition to *de facto* governments in Latin America if they are willing to assume former commitments and if they are not dominated by a foreign power.

Viewed by North American standards, a junta is acting in a constitutional void. Technically, in international usage, however, the possession of power may be all that is necessary to gain recognition. A constitution in the broad sense may indeed exist—that is, an effective government, at least for purposes of international intercourse.

Exile, Asylum, and Amnesty. In no other place in the world are the techniques of exile, asylum, and amnesty so frequently employed as in Latin America. The intense personalism that characterizes the political fray usually precludes any subsiding of emotion following a change involving force. Indeed, often in the orderly, electoral method of change, the loser accepts his loss only with the greatest difficulty. In a change brought about by force, exile is virtually a necessity. Almost always, arrangements have been made in advance, and exile is eagerly sought by the displaced leader and his chief assistants. In the more bitter situations, the executive will be sought as a criminal, and flight becomes an undeniable necessity. There is a tendency for exiles to gather in certain foreign cities; Cubans may gather in New York or Miami and Argentines in Montevideo; in Mexico City there are large numbers of disaffected Guatemalans.

During the Perón years, so many exiled Argentines were gathered in Montevideo that there flourished there an organization called the Argentine Exile Association. In Central America, so common are the exiles in a neighboring society that armies of invasion may apparently train undisturbed, or recruit friendly foreigners, for the triumphant "return" to the homeland. Thus, Castillo Armas was able to stage a substantial assault from Honduras back into his native Guatemala. A number of Costa Rican-Nicaraguan clashes in recent years have shown evidence of the strong touch of the exile. Indeed, so intimate are the relationships on these matters that former Costa Rican President Teodoro Picado while in exile in Nicaragua became the private secretary to the late President Anastasio Somoza.

In the years 1953 and 1954 there were two cases in the federal courts of the United States involving infractions of the United States' neutrality laws by Cubans or Cuban sympathizers; in the second case, former President Prío Socarrás was fined $9,000.00. In both cases were involved the buying and storing of munitions, presumably for eventual use against the Batista administration. The disaffected Cubans were also demonstrating considerable interest in a rather glamorous organization called the Caribbean Legion, which was presumably training to stage assaults upon a number of dictatorial regimes, the Dominican Republic in particular. The Legion was in training, allegedly, in Central America.

Before exile must come acceptance on the part of the host country. Thus the question of asylum arises. Ordinarily, asylum may be gained for important refugees in the embassy of another Latin American republic. Then, under safe conduct in accordance with international usage, the fugitive makes his way to the host country or perhaps to another country that has indicated willingness to accept him. Thus, Perón, upon his ouster, found safety on a Paraguayan gunboat; and, in spite of great protestations on the part of the new Argentine government, who were insistent upon holding him for trial as a criminal, Perón made his way to Paraguay and from there to the Dominican Republic.

The most celebrated case of asylum was that involving Haya de la Torre, leader of the *Apristas* in Peru, who won asylum in the Colombian embassy in Lima, in 1948, after some internal political difficulties.[8] The new Odría government complained determinedly that Haya was a common criminal and not entitled to privileges as a political refugee. The Colombians maintained just as determinedly that they would offer asylum. For over five years Haya was resident in the Colombian embassy, which was patrolled by Peruvian soldiers waiting for any attempt on the part of Haya to leave the Colombian sanctuary. In the meantime, two cases on the matter were heard before the International Court of Justice; in both, the decisions were sufficiently inconclusive for each side to claim the decision. Finally, Haya was allowed safe conduct to Mexico City in 1954.

In spite of considerable bitterness during the first phase of political overturn, most exiles are eventually granted amnesty and allowed to return home. This is frequently granted during the Christmas season as a gesture of the spirit of that season. It is thought that amnesty is at the same time a very practical gift, because the nature of the game is such that a president in power may be in need of similar treatment in the near future.

The "Cult of Violence"

In his final speech to the Mexican people, in 1946, President Camacho referred to the fact that he had labored to eliminate "the cult of violence." The subject of violence has engaged the attention of many writing about Latin America and, more broadly, Iberian culture. The Spaniard and his descendants in Latin America are often associated with passion, exaggerated pride, extreme sensitivity to personal dignity, and other similar postures or characteristics. Although one should resist the temptation to generalize, yet, the Latin American does demonstrate decided tendencies in these directions. Most observations indicate that the tendency to violence goes deeper than the immediate environment of nationalism and socio-economic aspirations. An extremist on the subject was undoubtedly García Calderón, who referred to "the African fanaticism which is satisfied only with excessive sensations and extreme solutions." [9]

Whether or not one accepts the generalization that the tendency to violence is a deep-seated cultural matter, the fact remains that there is much violence in Latin American public life.[10] Assassinations are fairly common; since the end of World War II these have involved presidents in Bolivia, Guatemala, Nicaragua, and Panama; a Mexican senator; a prominent leader of the Liberal Party in Colombia; a Guatemalan chief of staff; and a number of lesser figures. Many unsuccessful attempts are matters of record. On a provincial or local level, hundreds of other examples can be found.

The carrying of pistols appears fairly common in public life in some countries, even among highly placed figures.

In November 1946, the New York *Times* carried a picture of Rómulo Betancourt, presidential candidate in Venezuela, depositing his pistol before entering the polling place. Tempers flare in legislative chambers; the accounts of shootings in such circumstances are fairly frequent. Dueling is reported fairly often, particularly in Chile, Colombia, Cuba, and Peru. Two presidential candidates dueled in Chile in 1952. In no recent case, at least, has a duel resulted in serious injury; normally the test of courage is enough to satisfy both parties.

An extreme passion for martyrdom seems to characterize much of the violence. In 1954, President Vargas of Brazil shot himself after penning a very dramatic letter that brought about a short but exciting demonstration among his followers. Perhaps the most dramatic example of all was the martyrdom of Senator Eduardo Chibas of Cuba, the leader of the People's Party, who shot himself in August 1951, after finishing a radio address. In the trials of Batista followers following the Castro triumph, early in 1959 in Cuba, all the dramatic flourishes surrounding death in the public spotlight were in evidence; at one point in the trial of a high-ranking Batista army officer, a highly placed Castro henchman shouted that if this man were not convicted, he would kill himself. Followers are quick to make martyrs of their heroes, as was evidenced by the attempt of the Liberals in the Colombian Congress in 1948 to enact into legislation the "theses and doctrines" of Jorge Gaitán, their recently assassinated leader. Very frequently, candidates for martyrdom are students who demonstrate against the government in situations that may well result in violence. The disinclination of government to allow students to martyr themselves is indeed one of the reasons why students are very often granted concessions by a government that could perfectly well enforce its stand.

The possibility of violence stands in the foreground of important factors in public affairs. In the extreme, it appears in such quixotic and passionate form that there may well be a strong sense of preoccupation with violence

for the sake of violence on the part of many who undertake it or invite it.

Temptations of Power

In the image of Latin American politics, ranking with the
expectation of violence is the expectation of corruption in
public officials. Most Latin Americans are quite cynical
about equating ordinary morality with politics. Certainly
long experience, going back through the colonial period,
lends considerable support to this attitude. In most of the
republics, the belief is apparently strong that public officials
will enrich themselves in office.

The privilege of exercising political authority is likely
to be regarded as a concession. The most obvious evidence,
of course, is at the top, where quite clearly many presidents
and possibly some ministers become very wealthy persons
while in office. It is thought part of the game that a president will prepare for his future—a future that he may
have to spend in exile. Thus, enormous funds may have
been deposited in foreign banks or in foreign investment,
awaiting the day when they may prove to be useful. In
addition, of course, it is noticed that a president lives in
circumstances that far exceed his financial ability in terms
of his salary and expense account. It is almost never possible to be specific about such matters, but occasionally
some reports attempt to be and the amounts mentioned are
astonishing. Cuban politics offers some very good examples.
In 1951, former President Grau Martín was charged with
misappropriating one hundred seventy-four million dollars;
the ultimate indictment was for forty million, mainly
because valuable evidence was apparently stolen by gun-
men from a public office. Whether or not complete cre-
dence is to be given to such reports, they do give some
indication of the temptations involved. Many exiled presidents have been reported as living very handsomely indeed.
The latest one receiving appreciable attention in this
respect is Juan Perón of Argentina.

How are top officials able to siphon off substantial sums from the public coffers? All of the traditional "graft" techniques are undoubtedly employed—percentage cuts of contracts, the buying and selling of property that will shortly be used for substantial private or public development, and the like. One of the factors that explains the relative ease with which this may be carried off in many of the republics is the considerable power granted the president and national ministers with respect to budget matters. Typically, the power granted presidents includes very sweeping control over the revenues and allocations of public funds to administrative agencies. In addition to ordinary revenues, there are such temptations as lottery revenues and import duties. Furthermore, many of the republics operate large nationalized industries, the impact of which may be considerable on the total economy and involve enormous financial responsibilities. Since many of the republics have created national development agencies or centralized operations in foreign trade, there may be offered therein great temptation.

Also indicative of the "concession" approach to the dispensing of public services are the hundreds of minor ways in which lower officials may exact their "bite" (*mordida*), as it is called in Mexico. Seeking a license for any of many activities, a permit for construction, or some other service provided by lower levels of government may require paying the appropriate official; service will not ordinarily be forever denied without such a "fee" but quite likely the delay will be very long. It should be pointed out, although not for the purpose of condonation, that officials particularly at the lower levels are very poorly paid. To many of them, accepting money for their services differs not at all from the tipping required for excellent service in the restaurant. Thus, "government by tip" appears to be part of the pattern in much of Latin America and will endure until an improvement of the salary scales is accomplished.

The very best of intentions at the top may be unavailing with respect to "government by tip." When Ruiz Cortines took over the Mexican presidential office in 1953, he undertook a series of reforms to eliminate the *mordida*. Some officials were discharged; all public employees were required to submit financial reports; the president himself set the style by continuing his old simple life, refusing even to live in the presidential palace. Two results of this policy were immediately observed: at the top there was a dislocation that affected the economy, because the government operates a great part of business directly and is a large customer for other businesses; an enmeshing factor was now missing (or more cautiously applied); at the bottom, the risk was thought so great that the "fees" increased. In fairness to many other leaders in Latin America who have attempted reforms of this sort, it should be observed that it is very difficult to enforce such a program at the local level.

In a sense, the lack of political morality is related to the factor of violence in public life. Those who decide to seek political power feel that they are engaging in a game that may prove to be dangerous or at the very least temporary. They are inclined to exact payment for their disquietude.

CHAPTER FIVE

The Executive Power

In Latin American politics, the dominant institution is the presidency. Let us approach this focal institution by considering first the theoretical aspects and then the practical techniques by which the typical chief of state wins and maintains power.

In all systems, to some degree, the gap between theory and practice exists. By interpretation, which inevitably moves with the times, or by convention or custom, the stated form of government is altered. One must have considerable information to be able to read between the lines and see in realistic fashion the true operations of a system. The reading of constitutions and the observation of formal ceremony can be misleading. In a very real sense, no system is entirely what it appears to be; the reasons may differ widely, but difference there is. Relationships among men, in activating constitutions, create techniques that put the form in working order, as mere words cannot do. In some countries, this process merely involves supplementary apparatus (as the political party and the nominating process, not mentioned in the Constitution of the United States, determine the selection of the president); for others, it involves substantially altered processes that depart from the original (as in Great Britain, where the monarch is largely form and the cabinet and parliament are substance); for still others, there is also substantial alteration but in situations in which the original has never been applicable as a whole. In this last group fall the Latin American republics.

The Executive Power in Theory

The presidential form was brought forth in reaction to monarchy. It was designed to combine the advantage of unipersonal executive action inherited from monarchy and the limitations upon such action inherent in the ideas of popular sovereignty and consent of the governed. Thus, power tempered by accountability and based on selection rather than on inheritance was institutionalized.

The organization of a system that is basically a compromise between old and new and therefore seeks an equitable ratio of advantages to disadvantages is a most difficult and optimistic undertaking. The development of societies has not generally favored an easy solution. How does one design a system that provides power in certain respects as it restrains power in other respects? The solution of this problem lies squarely at the heart of political theory and political science. The presidential system was designed to give one man free rein to perform certain traditional functions of monarchy, within an area defined by constitution and laws, and in a manner not injurious to certain individual liberties of time-honored status—not a simple compromise. Jacques Necker, writing in 1791 as he witnessed the turmoil in France, observed:

The executive power is the moving force of a government. It represents, in the political system, that mysterious principle which, in moral man, unites action to the will. In the meantime so various are its relations, so extensive is its influence, and so great the pace, thus to express itself, which it occupies in the social order, that the adjustment of its limits, and the accurate adaptation of its means to its end, offer to the human mind one of the most comprehensive subjects of reflection.[1]

When we speak of the "presidential system," we may well be inviting confusion, for the title "president" is applied to an official in such continental cabinet systems as those of Italy, West Germany, and, until recently, France.[2] These presidential offices represent a much modified form of the presidential powers in the United States and in the Latin American republics. In actuality, they represent strong inclinations toward the elimination of the executive, only slightly modified by the necessity of providing some continuity independent of the tides of cabinet life.

Bearing in mind the extreme difficulties of adjusting the limits of executive power, even under favorable evolutionary circumstances, the cultural background of Latin America hardly seemed a salubrious climate for the nurture of presidential systems. As a matter of fact, the republics, as if recognizing this and providing a remedy, mixed with the presidential system some features intended to furnish a ministerial check upon executive action and, in a few instances, intended to provide some of the active machinery of cabinet responsibility. But these instruments failed, on the whole, to diminish a strongly intrenched inclination toward personal display of power.

Title. In the majority of the republics, the executive is given the official title of President of the Republic; a few add some designation of nationalism, such as President of the Argentine Nation or President of the Republic of Chile. A few constitutions add embellishments in such phrases as "Supreme Chief of the Nation" (Chile) or

"Supreme Head of the State" (Paraguay). On the whole, however, no extravagant phraseology is employed; in actuality, more extravagance usually would be necessary to indicate the true status of the executive.

In eight of the republics, we find descriptions of the executive power that tend to give a plural connotation (in Bolivia, Costa Rica, Colombia, Cuba, Guatemala, Panama, El Salvador, and Uruguay). The Costa Rican constitution of 1949 states that the executive power shall be exercised by "the President of the Republic and the Ministers of Government"; El Salvador's constitution of 1950 states: "The Executive Power shall be exercised by the President of the Republic and the Ministers and Under-Secretaries of State."

Uruguay. Uruguay recently adopted a system of organization of executive power unique in Latin America and very similar to that of Switzerland.[3] The executive power is organized in collegiate form and is called the National Council. It consists of nine councillors, who are responsible for executive action by majority vote. For ceremonial purposes, one of the councillors is named president for a one-year term, whereupon the title is passed in rotation among the other council members of the majority party.

Uruguay is, in many respects, a departure from the Latin American pattern, because it enjoys an intimate, homogeneous approach to many of the problems that are divisive elsewhere. It is, of course, a highly literate country; it has for generations enjoyed the reputation of being a most enlightened nation with great emphasis placed upon individual liberties.

Presidential Qualifications. A typical set of qualifications for the presidency includes: a person at least thirty years of age; a native son; and, in many cases, a resident for a certain number of years immediately preceding the election. Latin American republics have had a large number of young presidents, chiefly because of young military and intellectual leadership in times of crisis: Batista of Cuba, Pérez Jiménez of Venezuela, and Arbenz of Guatemala were all under forty when they first took office, just to name a sampling from recent years. A few republics require that the president be a Roman Catholic, not, of course, a serious limitation throughout Latin America; on the other hand, most republics require that the president be of the laity.

Generally there are a number of negative provisions that disqualify certain members of society. In addition to the barring of clergymen, the following prohibitions are frequently found: relatives of the incumbent president to perhaps the fourth degree of consanguinity, military officers on active duty, public officials who have held their posts within a certain period before the election, and a variety of morally deficient persons. With respect to restrictions aimed at public officials, resignations among those who might be considered presidential material are common in the months preceding an election.

Election and Terms of Office. Latin American presidents are elected by direct popular vote. (In the past, however, other methods were used, *e.g.*, the electoral college and congressional selection.) The typical requirement electorally is for an absolute majority or, failing this, congressional selection among the highest candidates. Official canvassing of the votes may be either by congress (as in Mexico) or by a high electoral jury or court.

And let us remember that, because *coup d'état* frequently enters the presidential electoral picture, a new constitutional congress frequently chooses the first president to start out under the new fundamental law.

The typical term of office is now six years, although some are four or five years. A very distinctive feature throughout Latin America has been the tenure limitation. All but four countries clearly deny immediate re-election, ten requiring the passage of at least one term before re-entering the picture, five extending this period of abstention to two terms. Mexico's constitution provides that no president may ever be re-elected. But a few republics have no limits at all on presidential tenure.

Line of Succession. Ten republics provide for the office of vice-president: Argentina, Bolivia, Brazil, Costa Rica, Chile, Cuba, Ecuador, Honduras, El Salvador, and Panama. Costa Rica and Panama each provide for two vice-presidents. The other republics have a variety of succession schemes. Some provide for succession by a particular minister; some by presiding officers of congress; and some simply by congressional selection.

Removal. For the removal of the president and other officers, the process of impeachment is possible in nearly all Latin American republics. The typical method is impeachment by the popular branch of the congress, followed by trial in the senate. In those republics with unicameral congresses, there is the possibility of the Supreme Court's playing a part.

Needless to say, the overpowering position of the president gives him little cause to fear impeachment himself, although he may see fit to use it against other officials.

Cabinets. Surrounding the president and constituting part of the executive branch are the ministers of state, who together are referred to as cabinets. In a number of the republics the relationship of the cabinet ministers to the congress has been described constitutionally in such a way as to indicate ministerial responsibility to the congress.[4] However, the ministers are not, in the first instance, members of congress; they may, in most cases, take part in some of the congressional deliberations, particularly those involving the presentation of legislation sponsored by the executive branch. The cabinet ministers are normally nominated by the president and approved by the senate; but they are nearly always removable at the pleasure of the president. The constitutions may mention specific ministries and attempt to enumerate the make-up of the cabinet (unlike the Constitution of the United States, which mentions nothing specifically about a "cabinet").

The Breadth of Presidential Power. In the delineation of power, the presidents of Latin American republics fall into the mold created by the constitution of the United States. Indeed, Latin American presidents are, in theory, ordinarily supplied with rather more than the sweep of power granted the president of the United States—to say nothing of practice. In actuality, as we shall see, they tend to fail of restraint and moderation, and thus the gap widens very critically between the two patterns.

The traditional executive powers are of course found in full measure—those powers that may be said to represent the direct inheritance of old monarchy. These powers, difficult to wield in representative bodies, remain part of the modern executive pattern everywhere. In this category would be found: the powers relating to pardon, commutation of sentence, and reprieve; the power of command over the armed forces; the power to appoint certain officials (perhaps shared with the legislative branch to some extent) and to remove certain officials; and the power to protect against invasion or to put down domestic violence. Calling for special mention in this group would be the power in foreign relations, an area in which executives have traditionally exercised such great influence, and, finally, the general responsibility, as administrative chiefs, over the functions of government established by legislative policy.

In the fiscal sphere, including both budgetary and fiscal policies, a typical Latin American executive is granted considerable power, much more than is granted to the president of the United States. In many cases, the executive can carry out a fiscal policy without legislative provision. If, for example, the congress fails to appropriate funds, the president may ordinarily continue to carry out the old program, including the tax levies, expenditures, and controls. In some cases, the president has acted entirely alone in this sphere for several years. Even under congressional approval and participation, the president usually does not have to submit to detailed itemizations and has considerable power over expenditures. Indeed, in this phase of executive power, one finds the explanation for many of the recriminations of presidential elections and particularly of those periods following the deposing of an executive.

In the so-called legislative powers, Latin American executives also can call into the fray a greater number of weapons in their relationships with the legislative branch. In essence, there exists a lesser degree of attachment to the separation of powers than is found in the United States. In addition to the usual influences regarding control (to some degree) of sessions, the delivering of messages, and the veto power, a typical president also has some degree of priority in the presentation of legislation and, as has been mentioned, has ministerial representation on the legislative floors during debate. In some republics, the executive is given sole right to the introduction of certain bills, such as appropriations and matters relating to administrative agencies. Finally, most executives engage more deeply in legislative matters through the use of "rules and regulations" than would be allowable in the United States, although much of this activity may indeed be by constitutional prescription.

Extraordinary Powers. Under the heading of "emergency," "national defense," or perhaps "public order," all Latin American constitutions empower presidents to act remedially. In most cases, such action involves congressional approval if congress is in session (or later, when it convenes), although this is usually not a strongly influential factor. The most common form of extraordinary power is the "state of siege" (already described in Chapter 2), by which constitutional rights may be temporarily set aside. Other forms exist, but in principle the motivations and actions are the same—the defense against assaults to the state and the preservation of order. Another extraordinary power is "intervention," particularly in federal systems (Argentina, Brazil, and Mexico, for example), by which, for essentially the same reasons, the government can intervene and, perhaps for a very long time, impose itself upon a subdivision of the state.[5]

The President in Action

Having surveyed certain of the cultural and socio-economic factors in Latin American life and having examined the theoretical framework within which executives operate, we may now combine these and investigate the real executive, winning power and maintaining it. To some extent, we have already touched upon the subject in discussing the practical side of government party activity with respect to the electoral process. The means by which power is won, whether constitutionally orderly or fraudulent, will on the whole indicate the pattern of the government in maintaining its power.

Loyalty lies at the center of the situation. In most of the republics, the president must be ever wary of his loyalty system—and loyalty in such an atmosphere is a great deal more than the mere loyalty of an administrator or of a voter.

Military Support. The loyalty of the armed forces is, of course, indispensable. The president cannot tolerate enemies in command positions in the armed forces. He will place staunch friends in such posts as those of Secretary of Defense (or War, Navy, etc.), Chief of Staff, and commanding officers of the principal garrisons, if he can do so without disturbing his original commitments. Loyal officers at lower levels may serve well by observing developments very closely in strategic locations. Many a *coup d'état* has been nipped by such a communications system. If the president is himself from the ranks of the military, he will ordinarily see to legislation very favorable to the armed services in terms of salary increases, promotions, and recreational facilities; and, furthermore, such a regime will frequently employ military personnel in civilian posts of government.

As an additional safeguard, and possibly a counterbalancing influence in time of need, a strongly organized and loyal police organization is a much cultivated weapon.

Friends and Relatives. As may be expected, Latin American public life is heavily laden with favoritism, even in the distribution of government posts. Government by cronies (*amiguismo*) is very highly developed in the smaller republics in particular. Nepotism is widespread and, again, is most common in the smaller republics; one family in, say, the Dominican Republic or Nicaragua can be found in many public posts and in the favored business locations as well. Family loyalty is of course a characteristic cultural factor among Latins. Furthermore, the "family" includes a very large number of distantly connected relatives, many affiliated by marriage only, and also godparents and godchildren. The fact that constitutions frequently take the trouble to bar from high office relatives of the incumbent to remote degrees attests to the impact of family on public affairs.

Excessive Sensitiveness. In keeping with the cultural emphasis on personal dignity and pride, Latin American presidents are ordinarily exceedingly sensitive to personal affronts that would be considered "part of the game" elsewhere. And, in many cases, the personal affront may be nothing more than just opposition. Thus, there is likely to be legislation to protect the president from "disrespect" (*desacato*). There is more sensitivity in some countries than others on this point; much depends, too, on the delicacy of the power structure that the president must maintain. A very sensitive regime can usually invoke such legislation to silence opposition. A hard-hitting article in a newspaper or magazine, a speech delivered during a political rally, even actors providing entertainment can sometimes be punished for offending the dignity of the president. Opposition leaders may be jailed for alleged "disrespect" and find themselves still incarcerated at election time. The Perón administration, for example, was sensitive to such a point that a prominent opposition leader in the congress was sentenced to prison for "disrespect." As mentioned in an earlier chapter, duels are common among prominent politicians, even presidential candidates.

The Opposition. Opposition in general is difficult for Latin American presidents to endure. Opposition is very likely to be considered treason or subversion. There are countries, to be sure, where it is allowed—as in Argentina at the moment, Brazil, Chile, Costa Rica, Ecuador, Mexico. On the whole, however, and even in these republics, there is a decided intolerance for opposition.

It is difficult for the opposition to determine what amount and intensity of opposition will be suffered by the government. Perhaps the vaguest standard was set by President Farrell of Argentina, who, in 1945, stated that only "noble criticism" was justified. What would "noble criticism" be? Very likely it would involve, first of all, some indication of loyalty. Then, perhaps, its tone might well have to be that of suggestion for action rather than castigation of those in power. It would stick to an impersonal discourse on "things" rather than "people." Doubtless it would be interpreted to mean any calm recitation that could not possibly offend dignity and pride. For in a system based to such degree on personalism, the person of the President is thought inviolate by himself and his followers. In short, "noble criticism" would probably best be translated as "kindly suggestion."

There is a tendency to think of "mandate" not only as the right to govern for a fixed term but also as the right to govern without annoying opposition. Frequently a militant opposition will be considered the possible first stage of an attempt to unseat the government.

As a result of these tendencies, the opposition in many republics is severely limited. Laws affecting the press, radio, and speech are often severe or at least so loosely drawn as to allow rather liberal interpretation. In March 1954, three editors of a Chilean publication were sent to prison for criticism of the government and were later banished for a time to a remote southern province. The closing down of *La Prensa* in Buenos Aires by the Perón administration was perhaps one of the outstanding examples in recent years. In this assault, the government pressed a campaign against *La Prensa* that first attempted to withhold newsprint, then closed the establishment for reasons of sanitation, and finally seized the paper outright after a news vendors' strike. In Colombia, in 1954, a government decree on press reporting stated that only "factual" reporting on political matters would be allowed; such phrases as "it is reported" or "it is rumored" were illegal.

Administration of Public Affairs. In spite of the many signs of ministerial checks upon the president and the occasional structure of congressional action against ministers, the president in fact controls the system. The cabinets in Latin America, with very few exceptions, are quite like the cabinet in the United States—responsible in fact to executive will. When difficulty is encountered, the president is usually able to realign his team and start out once more. Even in those republics where a large number of parties exist and the president has been selected by virtue of a "front" made up of several, all having their own representation in the congress, the president is usually not severely handicapped. The fact that most legislative sessions are short, leaving the president with a clear field for action for a substantial portion of the year, is an important factor in support of presidential supremacy. The only really successful application of strong congressionalism was in Chile from 1891 to 1925, during which time an effective parliamentary system operated. Chile remains, indeed, a republic in which the president is much more dependent upon congressional support than in most of the other republics.

Cabinet changes are very frequent in all of Latin America, although only occasionally as a result of congressional action. One of the most common motivations has been economic in the form of inflation, unemployment, with ensuing labor unrest. At such times, appropriate ministers may resign (or be removed). Cabinet changes are particularly frequent in those republics with multiparty systems, in which coalitions may have been necessary to elect the president (at various times, Bolivia, Chile, Ecuador, Panama, Peru). The coalitions are so fluid in nature that, after success in the election and upon meeting a divisive problem, they frequently develop a conflict out of tune with the original agreement. There is a very great likelihood of this happening before the end of the president's term since the coalitions in reality have substance only for the presidential election and no real pretence of durability based on issues.

At the approach of a new election, cabinet changes are common. Some of the ministers may themselves be prospective candidates for presidential office and thus want to give the impression that they will not use their offices to further their chances; sometimes, indeed, the law requires such resignations. Other ministers may leave simply to release themselves from commitments. The president may want to give the impression of providing "neutral" cabinet members. Occasionally, a "technical cabinet" will be organized at such times—or earlier in critical circumstances; such a group usually consists of undersecretaries or professionals outside of the bureaucracy.

Although much improvement is being made in some republics, public administration is not a well-developed science in Latin America. Aside from the difficulties that the political environment presents, there are basic problems relating to the availability of skilled technicians and also the inevitable pattern of poor pay and uncertain internal personnel administration. The spoils system is widely practiced; as already observed, the struggle for power is very much associated with the striving for livelihood in the form of bureaucratic positions. To a very considerable degree, this lack is but a special variation of the domination of the executive. Altogether too much dependence upon presidential leadership is a notable failing in public administration, particularly in fiscal matters.

Legislative Powers. Most observers of Latin American government agree that it is the president who legislates and the congress that vetoes (and vetoes only with temporary results usually). As we have seen, even in theory, the president is a very powerful co-legislator; in practice, he may outstrip the constitutional prescription. In his legislative role, we find him displaying one of the most characteristic of authoritarian tendencies: he usually creates policy as well as executes it. In all but a few cases, the president commands the legislative branch through his followers or, lacking sufficient followers, through the raw power of his office. By far the greater time is taken up with administration-sponsored measures and, as we have seen, usually under the direct supervision of the president's ministers.

The president can usually control the sessions of congress by a number of techniques. If he commands the majority party, there will be no problem; the majority may be so zealous as not to extend the usual courtesies to opposition. It is not unknown for the majority, by absenting itself, to prevent a quorum and thus forestall any business and, by inaction, silence the opposition. Occasionally a strong majority will wield its powers of expulsion (normally requiring a two-thirds vote). This same majority can usually be employed to amend the constitution. If all else fails, there is always the possibility of direct executive action in consequence of "emergency" powers. In a few republics, the power of the president under certain circumstances extends to proroguing the congressional session.

Decrees. One of the most direct means of dominating the legislative branch is that of usurpation of lawmaking power by executive decree. This has been carried to extraordinary lengths in some republics, particularly in the void presented by a change of government through *coup d'état*. Some distinctions need to be made among various forms of decrees.[6] In general there are two kinds, decrees (*decretos*) and decree-laws (*decreto-leyes*), although there is occasionally some confusion in the use of these terms. All executives in all systems have a certain amount of rule-making power, of course, necessary for administrative convenience in carrying out policy determined in the legislative branch. In Latin American parlance, this mild and universally used decree power would be referred to as *potestad reglamentaria* (rule-making power). Other decrees are possible through direct stipulation of the constitution, given to the executive specifically in some particular area of action: *reglamentos autonomos* (autonomous rules). In the employment of both these decrees, the executive may of course go beyond a reasonable interpretation of intent, perhaps to the alteration of legislative or constitutional intent rather than to the administration of it.

The decree-law offers broad possibilities. It is an inheritance from continental usage, forged in an essentially strong monarchic atmosphere rather than, for example, the stronger parliamentary atmosphere of Great Britain. The basic laws of France, for example, have always provided this outlet for executive action, under emergency conditions. In Latin America, the decree-law can make its appearance in several ways. It may be delegated to the executive by the legislative branch in order to handle a severe crisis, such as an economic disaster. It may be provided by the constitution in circumstances of dire emergency—in theory, a situation in which the regular legislative channels would be ineffective. Or, finally, it may simply be employed by the executive in a situation of his own making—essentially an extra-constitutional use of raw power, as, for example, following a *coup,* which in effect frequently suspends the constitution. In some instances, the executive branch has ruled without congress for years: President Morínigo did so in Paraguay from 1943 to 1947; no Colombian congress met for several years during the civil disturbances following 1948; in Argentina, following the *coup* of 1930, the decree-laws filled several volumes.

Emergency Powers. The emergency powers with which the Latin American president is armed, under conditions defined by constitutions, may on occasion be interpreted so loosely and be put in action so frequently that they become ordinary weapons in the political struggle. The state of siege, the intervention power, the emergency decree powers—these may be employed to effect a certain political gain rather than to protect the nation as originally intended. In Argentina, for example, it has been a traditional political move, after a change in the power structure, to intervene in all the provinces in order to reshape them into the new regime. Also, such intervention may be effected at a later time in order to influence a coming election.

"Power Corrupts"

Political power is everywhere a stern master. Under the most desirable of conditions, the realities of governing are such as to create a gap between the "ought to be" and "is." Not only the mere presence of power, but also the time-consuming minutiae of maintaining power leave less time for the fulfillment of ideals than even the most hopeful of power-wielders expects. And in Latin America are to be found all the most aggravating influences that make closing the gap difficult. The problems are massive and often appear impossible to solve within a reasonable planning period. The temptations of power are exceedingly great, the possibilities of enrichment fantastic in scope. The loyalty that one must command is an expensive luxury and always dubious in its constancy.

In only a minority of the republics have there developed trends that seem strongly disposed to override these considerations, although all of them will undoubtedly do so in time.

CHAPTER SIX

Presidents, *Caudillos,* and Guardians

One of the terms most frequently used in popular parlance about Latin American affairs has been "dictator." Indeed, it is applied so freely that it has become misleading; such seems to be the tendency in the language of politics—a tendency to stretch one word far beyond its real content. It might be well, therefore, to attempt some clarification of the nature of authoritarianism in Latin America and, in particular, to classify presidential types in order to make possible greater precision.

The Nature of New World Authoritarianism

The experience of the past two decades has brought into comparative government (and into social studies in general) a considerable emphasis on authoritarianism. The spectacular and extreme versions represented by the Hitler and Mussolini systems undoubtedly gave great impetus to this emphasis. In addition to the investigation of the nature of the over-all pattern, there have also been attempts to establish distinctions; it is necessary to realize that, while totalitarian systems are extreme examples of authoritarianism, highly authoritarian systems can exist without all the overwhelming machinery and oppressive techniques of the totalitarian state.[1] The concern to maintain distinctions has been deepened by the increasing and alarming tendency in these postwar years to group rather too easily—or to polarize—into neat little ideological packages. In the study of Latin American systems, it is vital to distinguish degrees of authoritarianism. Indeed, the first observation that needs to be made is that no Latin American system, however loftily a leader may have ascended within it, has been classifiable as a totalitarian state.

There is no doubt about the deeply ingrained authoritarianism in the Iberian culture or the tendency of this characteristic to cling in Latin America. But authoritarianism in the New World is significantly different from the Old World Iberian pattern. The distinctions do not lie in such cultural trappings as Church, family, or personalism; these tend to be very much the same. The real distinctions are historical in nature, functions of time and space, rather than of basic cultural patterns.

The basic difference between the Old World and New World Iberian authoritarianism centers on a vital factor in history—*revolutionary commitment.* In critical periods when national sentiment is directed to revolution, and particularly when important institutional changes are sought, the ideals and institutions for which the revolution is fought constitute a commitment that will dictate the form, if not always the substance, of that nation for a very long period of time. Next to natural historical growth (such as custom's place in the growth of law), this may well be the most compelling institutional and ideological determinant. If the substance is appreciable (as in the United States), a high degree of consistency to the commitment may be maintained; if the substance is meager, the form will nevertheless be employed to await the growth of substance.

The Latin American republics, unlike such seats of Old World authoritarianism as Spain and Portugal, have a revolutionary commitment to the ideals and institutions of responsible, representative democracy of the presidential type. The consistency displayed varies considerably from republic to republic, but even in republics where substance may be long in developing, the revolutionary commitment is compelling and is a major institutional determinant.

One of the most common manifestations of Latin American commitment is the compulsion to seek legality by constitution, even if power is won and maintained extra-constitutionally. No Latin American president rests comfortably in power without eventually seeking constitutional status, if he ascended to power without it. A good deal of the addiction to constitution-making in Latin America is attributable to this compulsion.

It would appear in the face of these observations that a significant factor in comparative government is often overlooked—the environmental impact of institutions *per se*. Generally speaking, most students of comparative government emphasize the necessity of immersing themselves in the culture in order to understand properly political institutions. A corollary is that one wastes time inspecting institutions for any value in themselves. There is a danger of overemphasis of this downgrading of institutions. For institutions *per se* may be influences as well as mere results. This is clear in Latin America, where, if it may be argued that the presidential system was too abruptly adopted, generations of Latin Americans have stuck doggedly to the form—the commitment—until it has become a firm piece of continuous environmental influence.

Another distinction between Old World and New World authoritarianism, another function of time and space, is the separation from the old order of Europe. This has created a spirit of innovation, a feeling of creativeness, institutionally speaking. It has accounted for a very decided sense of constructiveness, of society in motion; this sense can, of course, develop action both for progress or for withdrawal. A Latin American republic is always faced with a wide range of choices, and nowhere is this more evident than in the activities of the executive power.

All these factors, considered in combination, constitute an introduction to the essence of the relationship between Latin American executive power and executive power in general. From this basis one can begin the investigation of the differences in degree that have developed. Let us now attempt a classification of Latin American executives, based on patterns that have been distinguishable, particularly in the last twenty-five years.

Major Types of Latin American Executives

Before investigating these classifications it would be well to stipulate two assumptions upon which the approach rests. First, it should be assumed that the Latin American presidencies are offices with historical depth in accordance with the principle of commitment mentioned above; we are not discussing useless and fleeting institutions. Second, it is assumed that standards applied with the United States in mind are unrealistic; all executives in Latin America are to some degree illustrative of authoritarianism in the Iberian tradition; all the ordinary evidences of *personalismo* are taken for granted as characteristic of even the most responsible presidents.

1. *Constitutional President.* Perhaps the most distinguishing feature of the constitutional president is that he has existed in greater numbers than is widely believed. As we mentioned before, one of the most commonly used terms with reference to Latin American politics is "dictator." To be sure, there have been many of these through the years, but there have also been a great many presidents who have taken over and carried out official duties within reasonable reach of constitutional directives.

A number of conditions are necessary to inclusion in this classification. Election must be constitutionally acceptable, a reasonable reflection of the popular will (taking into consideration the retardation in such a matter as suffrage and the reality of public opinion that exists in many republics). It must be understood that this condition does not bar the eventual constitutionality of a regime initially established by *coup d'état*. Establishment of power by force may be necessary to the fulfillment of constitutional conditions. At a suitable time thereafter, however, legitimation of a proper sort must follow. It is not easy to assess the propriety of these steps in all cases. When is a *coup* legitimized properly, and when is it legitimized under intimidation, for example? There is no sure formula widely applicable. One can perhaps safely judge that the legitimization of the National Revolutionary Movement in 1952, when Paz Estenssoro took over the presidency, reflected a genuinely popular sentiment, since he had received a plurality of votes cast in the election at issue.[2] On the other hand, Batista legitimized himself in 1954 with strong intimidation of Cuban opposition groups that left considerable doubt as to genuineness. A government of dubious status itself can pave the way for a constitutional regime. For example, General Odría's government, established by force in Peru in 1948, and later supposedly legitimized by an election in 1950, made its way under the shadow of a suppressed popular party (the *Apristas*); by 1956, however, this party was allowed some freedom, and the election of Manuel Prado qualifies, in the main, as a constitutionally proper one.

To satisfy the requirements of this type, it is also necessary that freedom be allowed the opposition to contest elections reasonably effectively and to express opposition to policy-making as well. Again, we encounter difficulty of interpretation, and we must resort to a realistic appraisal of local circumstances. Thus, in spite of the opposition's continuous cry of fraud and *imposición,* the PRI in Mexico must be granted legitimacy in these respects. The PRI must be viewed for what it is—a very large confederation of political groups, within which the ordinary differences of politics are fought out, similar to the Democratic party in some southern states. There is a very considerable difference between the PRI and the *Colorados* of Paraguay or the *Partido Dominicano* of the Dominican Republic, to mention the other major examples of one-party domination in the Latin American area. It is a difference that touches on the aspects of the formation of opposition, from effective party organization to the various phases of the electoral process and including the expression of opposition effectively in the various media of communication. A crucial criterion is, of course, the application of laws affecting the freedom of expression in its many forms.

The fraternity of constitutional presidents does not include those executives who have unreasonably maneuvered constitutions to extend their tenure of office beyond the original spirit of the constitution. The practice of *continuismo* is not in harmony with Latin American constitutionalism, and it is particularly disqualifying when it involves that version by which a president-dominated constitutional assembly, after drawing up a new fundamental law, proceeds to appoint the incumbent as the president to serve under the new system.[3] This disqualification does not extend, of course, to a proper constitutional amendment relating to extension of tenure if the incumbent is then elected to the office.

Finally, it should be observed that to occupy the post of constitutional president, personalism must be confined to constitutional limits. When a president, however legitimate originally, climbs aloft to a pedestal and creates a level for himself above the constitution, particularly if he actively sponsors a cult centering on his person, he has violated the spirit of Western constitutionalism. The constitutional president must be conscious of his heritage in this respect and exercise restraint.

There is a very strong correlation between the greater number of constitutional presidents and the greater political awareness evident among the great mass of people in those republics. This awareness is in turn dependent on well-known social, economic, and educational advantages. The most constant of these have been Chile, Costa Rica, Mexico, and Uruguay.[4] Standing in secondary rank are Argentina, Brazil, Colombia, and Cuba. Ecuador, Guatemala, Peru, El Salvador, and Venezuela have shown occasional promise; Bolivia appears to be enjoying an introduction.

2. *Demagogic* Caudillo. The demagogic *caudillo* has not as yet appeared in quantity, but he represents a highly spectacular type that warrants attention because of the very modern touch involved. It bears some similarities to European fascism, although generally it is not properly classifiable as such. There are a number of distinguishing features that serve to give this type a standing of its own. Argentina, during the years when Juan Perón dominated the scene, affords the best example.[5]

The first characteristic of the demagogic *caudillo* is a very close relationship to constitutionalism. The type emerges in a system that has had deep commitments to constitutional presidencies in the past. The demagogic *caudillo* can easily win legitimation by elections. He rises above constitutionalism not necessarily by violation of electoral laws but chiefly on personal grounds. The proper location of this type is the republic with a high degree of political awareness founded on an economic order of considerable productivity. A key to the power structure created is a large industrial workers' movement of such massive power that it becomes an aggressive reflection of popular support. The movement must be constantly wooed and rewarded, even to a point beyond the attention customarily given to the military. The demagogic *caudillo* realizes the harnessing of a force which transcends the military and which, until the structure weakens, can be used effectively to stand off strong military opposition. The maintenance of such a mass system of approval calls for extraordinary powers of organization, diversion, and communication. One of the weaknesses of the system is the difficulty of keeping mass support alive, for it has an appetite that grows and becomes increasingly difficult to satisfy. Since the leader has committed himself to the role of savior of the worker and since increasing adulation of him soon transcends the more mundane spirit of the constitution, the cult of the Leader results. It is this characteristic that most closely resembles the European totalitarian systems of recent memory.

Excessive nationalism, with the implication that Latin American leadership is involved, along with very heavy doses of anti-Yankeeism, is very important to the pattern. One of the distinctive touches is ideological in nature. The Leader becomes the symbol of an ideology—preferably a "new way," like the supposedly new course struck by Perón's *justicialismo*. The demagogic *caudillo* takes the old complaints and declares that he has solved them by a quasi-messianic summoning of the greatness of the people.

The demagogic *caudillo* represents a curious combination of regression and advancement. He is of both worlds, Old and New. He is regressive in that he builds firmly upon ingrained authoritarianism and creates a gigantic monument to personal leadership; but he is a symbol of advancement in that he has realistically appraised a modern industrial society, wooed and won mass support, and undertaken a social mission in keeping with the twentieth century's demands.

The prototype is Juan Perón. (Vargas of the 1930's merits some consideration, but his claim to real legitimation was rather poorly founded until his return in 1950.) Perón was popularly elected in 1946 and again in 1952, and it is clear that he would probably have been elected on both occasions even without the intimidations practiced by a very enthusiastic party following. He was raised to heroic stature and from this eminence he clearly operated beyond the intentions of the constitution. It would not be correct to label Perón as the product solely of Latin American caesarism, or as the *duce* of a totalitarian system, or even as a military dictator. He was each of

these in some measure, but principally he represents a
new departure—a leader with all the characteristics of a
constitutional president, who, however, soared out of the
constitutional cage into a personal venture so high as to
allow for no safe return.

At the moment, there is no demagogic *caudillo* in any of
the republics. If one were to explore potentialities and
risk speculation, there appears only one possible candidacy
and there are many reasons why it might not develop.
This possibility is Fidel Castro of Cuba. Cuba fits the
pattern fairly well in terms of socio-economic pressures
reflected in voluble mass sentiments. It lacks the major
ranking that could justify pretensions to Latin American
leadership, but this could be overweighed by the stature
of Castro as a revolutionary leader already with considerable heroic stature. Castro could ascend to dizzy
heights of personalism in the circumstances, particularly if
there could be added some of the provocations that attended
the rise of Perón in Argentina.

3. *Military Guardian.* The setting for the military guardian
is the republic of major or medium power in economic
terms, wherein an appreciable—if not substantial—political
awareness has been generated. Usually, the political scene
has been sufficiently active to provide for a number of
political parties. One of these parties may be the vehicle
of considerable popular sentiment for reform; its strength
is potentially great enough to make a bid for power and,
indeed, it may have done so only to be thwarted by perhaps illegal methods. One of the sociological factors of
this setting is invariably the lack of a large middle class
actively seeking change. In such a sociological situation,
the military has usually flourished as a political determinant. In the period since the end of World War II, excellent examples have been found in Colombia, Peru, and
Venezuela.

Against this general background may be viewed the
various thought patterns of the military officer intent upon

political power. Military guardians arise in an endless variety of combinations of local political considerations, but there are two major justifications cited by intervening military leaders that demand particular attention: order and neutralism. Ordinarily, these are found in combination, and they are very closely related. Order is, of course, a major preoccupation of the military profession everywhere. In Latin American republics, there occur many opportunities for using it as a justification, although often the intervention of the military goes well beyond the demands of the situation. One of the best examples of military guardianship set up in the name of order was that of General Rojas Pinilla in Colombia in 1953. Colombia had for generations enjoyed comparatively orderly government without military intervention. The bitter struggle between the Liberals and the Conservatives broke out into widespread violence following the assassination of a Liberal leader, Gaitán, in 1948. This soon assumed the magnitude of civil war, with apparently little chance of bringing the warring political leaders to settlement. Breaking a tradition of very long standing, General Rojas Pinilla stepped in and took over power. There were other, personal motivations involved, but essentially some movement toward order was necessary. Once in power, General Rojas Pinilla was motivated by power itself and carried intervention to a point not justified by the situation.

More common in the ranks of military guardianship is the complicated motivation that might be said to result in a defensive military guardian. In this maneuver, neutralism is cited in order to protect the national dignity, honor, and traditions from the excesses of the masses. Stated more baldly, this is a last stand against popular government that threatens the old order. A large popular party presses forward with the electoral power to sweep into office; the language of reform fills the air. The military guardian comes forward to "save" the republic from this mass "chaos." The best recent examples were in Peru and Venezuela, where the *Apristas* and Democratic Action, re-

spectively, had demonstrated enough power to win elections. Accordingly, General Odría in Peru and Colonel
Pérez Jiménez in Venezuela intervened and suppressed the
parties battering at the gates. Both leaders said that it was
time to save the masses from their own ignorance, or words
similar in meaning. General Odría, indeed, stated this
most colorfully when he announced that "party politics
poisons the hearts of the people and sickens their minds." [6]
One is reminded of Thomas the Cynic, in Ignazio Silone's
School for Dictators, who stated that in socially backward
countries "the army constitutes the only barrier against the
so-called 'anarchy' of the popular masses and the corruption of the politicians." [7] This belief has been enter-
tained by many Latin American military guardians. The
stated aim is "neutralism," but the result is suppression of
popular will. A special version of this sort of guardianship took place in Guatemala in 1954, when Castillo Armas
swept in to remove the impact of Communism as it was
supposedly represented by President Arbenz.

All the military guardians are, of course, driven by some
degree of personal yearning for power. The military-officer
class in a typical Latin American republic is a considerable
reservoir of political ambitions. A leader among them may
be given an opportunity sooner or later to cite one of the
ancient justifications for military intervention and thus
launch a political career at the head of the republic.
The military guardian, in our time, stands ultimately at
the mercy of the popular movement he wishes to delay.
Both Odría and Pérez Jiménez have given way to constitutional presidents, although the circumstances of their
withdrawal differ considerably; Odría presided over an
election and Pérez Jiménez was ousted from office.

4. *Paternalistic* Caudillo. In the paternalistic *caudillo* we
find a type that was more widely evident in the nineteenth
century, before the onset of industrialism and associated
effects. At the present time, it is narrowed down largely to
the Central American and Caribbean areas, particularly

the Dominican Republic and Nicaragua. Although a special case, Paraguay belongs in this category. A decade or two ago the paternalistic *caudillo* flourished in most of the Central American republics in very spectacular fashion. As the name indicates, the system of government resembles a large *hacienda* with a very strong superimposition of the *patrón*.

The paternalistic *caudillo* is, indeed, a national *patrón*. He may in fact possess large holdings in property and control a number of basic industries. Nepotism is especially evident in such a system; the total holdings of the *caudillo*'s family connection will be staggering. The paternalistic *caudillo* carries to an extreme a long-entertained notion in Latin American political life: the possession of political power is a concession and the concessionaire manages as large a return as possible (much of which may be quite legal—"honest graft," as it is sometimes called in the United States). The republic is in great part a private preserve. The *caudillo* need not be overpoweringly oppressive, although he protects his system with very tightly controlled military forces. He may be viewed by many as a great national father who takes care of his own, at least to the extent he feels is good for them. The *caudillo* usually openly indicates that he is exercising tutelage over ignorant and childlike people who are not ready for all the bewildering machinery of a free system. Some of the major examples of recent years have been the following: Anastasio Somoza, who, until his assassination in 1957, ruled Nicaragua for approximately 20 years (and left his "plantation" in the hands of two sons); Rafael Trujillo of the Dominican Republic, who has dominated that country for 29 years; and Tiburcio Carías Andino, who dominated Honduras for 17 years until 1949. In Venezuela, the last of the larger republics to support a paternalistic *caudillo*, Juan Vicente Gómez managed to rule for 27 years, until his death in 1935.

There are two electoral features that characterize the administrations of paternalistic *caudillos*. The technique of

continuismo is employed to excess in such circumstances—
that is, the application of presidential domination to extend
one's tenure beyond the intention of the constitution. The
other feature has to do with alternation in office. A paternalistic *caudillo*'s position is usually so secure that he can
occasionally afford the luxury of allowing someone else
a turn in the presidential office, perhaps a member of the
family (like Hector Trujillo, brother of Rafael).

Provisional Executive Arrangements. Because at any given
time at least one republic has recently undergone a *coup*
or some other interruption of the constitutional pattern,
brief mention should be made of a very significant Latin
American executive organization, the provisional government. The most common institution is the junta, a council
made up of a varying number of revolutionaries, usually
not more than five. The junta's aim is to provide temporary
leadership until the constitutional electoral process can
be reinstituted. It may be several years before the provisional government deems it proper to hold such an election. In the meantime, a constitutional assembly may be
reworking the constitution, which will serve as the banner
of "the new era." Another provisional arrangement is to
continue the presidential office, but with a president appointed by the successful revolutionary leadership. Cuba
set up this system in 1959, with a front man as president and Fidel Castro, the leader of the revolutionary
movement, assuming the office of prime minister.

Since it may be said that provisional government is in
great measure government exercised in a constitutional
void, it must be observed that from this position the leader
of a *coup* may go in any one of several directions. He may,
of course, simply provide for the resumption of constitutional activity in a short time without unnecessarily in-
fluencing the process, as appears to have happened in
Argentina preceding the election of President Frondizi. He
may employ his position to create electoral triumph for
himself in due time, as witness Batista in the Cuban elec-

tion of 1954. He may simply ignore the electoral process and establish himself arbitrarily in a presidential term of office either by a "plebiscite," as did Castillo Armas in Guatemala following the coup of 1954, or by arranging his appointment by a hand-picked constitutional assembly, as was demonstrated by Vargas on the occasion of the 1934 constitution.

CHAPTER SEVEN

The Subsidiary Legislative and Judicial Powers

If there be validity to the notion that responsible modern government is a result of the diminution of old authoritarian patterns, then the institution that best reflects it is the legislature. If the legislative body is a real force—independent and vigorous—the nation developing it is a full partner in the select company of effective modern representative systems. For what unlimited executives have lost, the legislature and, to some extent, the judiciary and the people have gained. This shift of power has focused on the legislature, where policy must be formed and the very difficult art of compromise practiced. It might be said that authoritarianism is easy and natural but that the responsible representative system is difficult and demanding.

The Legislative Power[1]

Surely one of the elements of the Latin American pattern of government that shows the least variation from republic to republic is the decidedly secondary position of the legislative power. Except for brief flourishes in a few republics —particularly in Chile—Latin American legislative bodies have never achieved the power of the congress of the United States. The executive power is normally in a position to call the tune.

Structure. Fourteen of the Latin American legislative bodies are bicameral; only Costa Rica, Guatemala, Honduras, Panama, Paraguay, and El Salvador employ the unicameral form. In the bicameral bodies, the title "Senate" is universally used for the upper houses, and the typical title for the lower house is "Chamber of Deputies." Direct popular election is involved in the selection of members, either by the single-member district system or a rich variety of proportional representation schemes for multi-member districts. In Ecuador, a number of "functional" senators are designated by the groups represented: education, both public and private; journalism and scientific and literary societies; agriculture; commerce and unions; and others. Terms of office vary: four-, five-, or six-year terms are common for upper houses, with perhaps the same or less for lower houses. It is usual to elect alternates at the same time in order to provide for vacancies. In the republics where the multi-party system prevails, there may be a bewildering number of party lists in a typical election in spite of the tendency to form alliances for the selection of the president.

Sessions. Legislative sessions in Latin America are typically of only a few months' duration, a fact which tends to heighten the supremacy of the executive during the greater part of the year. A typical session is four months long, and during a good part of that time the sittings may be short, perhaps only a few hours per day.

Frequently, either by virtue of the wish of the majority to silence the minority or the wish of the minority to prevent action, quorums may be lacking, in which case business cannot be transacted. A common occurrence is the planned boycott of the sessions immediately following elections in order to give an opportunity for the losers to hamper the majority. This may have an added significance —the absence of sufficient opposition numbers may make it impossible to make the final canvass of ballots and thus officially elect a president. One of the most spectacular of such boycotts took place in Honduras in 1954, when two factions of the Nationalist Party refused to meet in the legislative session necessary to select the president who had headed the Liberal ticket. In Argentina, during the Perón years, there were occasions when the *Peronistas* in the Chamber of Deputies absented themselves in order to spare themselves the bitter opposition of the Radicals.

In extreme form, there are periods when the legislature meets not at all. This is usually the result of a situation in which the executive has assumed total powers in varying circumstances. It happened, for example, in Paraguay when, under President Morínigo, there were no congressional meetings for a period of approximately five years. More often this happens in the void following a *coup d'état*, as in Venezuela from 1948 to 1953.

Organization and Procedure. The rules of organization and procedure have a certain uniformity. A typical Latin American legislative chamber elects a president and other officers; in a few republics, this choice is of considerable significance, because the presidential succession may, at least temporarily, fall to the presiding officer of one of the chambers. There are usually two vice-presidents. Standing committees are selected usually with some attention to proportional representation based on party strength, where this is a real factor.

The legislative process is chiefly distinguished by its favoring of presidential bills (usually by virtue of special priority) and by the participation of ministers in the legislative procedure (usually without voting power). It is normal procedure to follow the continental method of passing upon a bill in principle before moving on to the consideration of details.

Decorum. Occasionally violence occurs during the meetings of the congress. In the last few years such episodes have been reported from Colombia and Ecuador, for example, several times each. In Colombia, September 1949, in the early phase of the vicious civil disturbance that lasted several years, a representative was killed in a gun fight in the house of representatives; three others were reported wounded. On the less violent side, there are frequently debates that demonstrate high emotionalism. Occasionally, as in Peru recently, the result of such a clash is a duel between the two members whose respective dignities were apparently most damaged.

There is occasional use of the expulsion procedure. Because, in a number of republics, the majority party can usually summon and receive the typical two-thirds majority required, the too-militant minority leader may face expulsion proceedings. In Argentina, during the Perón years, when at least two-thirds of the members of the chamber of deputies were of the majority party (the senate, unanimously Peronist, was not involved), much activity of this sort was observed.

The typical session, of course, is orderly. Indeed, it may be so much dominated by the government group as to sacrifice adequately considered legislation.

Checking the Executive Power. As already intimated, the typical Latin American congress does not in reality exercise effectively the constitutional assignment to check the activity of the executive. In a few republics, for example, Chile, Cuba, and Guatemala, this has been done sporadically. In Chile there have been times when the congress has been able to take a vigorous anti-presidential attitude and achieve some results. The fact that there existed an effective parliamentary system in Chile from 1891 to 1925 provides some of the momentum for this comparatively spectacular display of legislative independence. In 1954, after much flinging of charges back and forth between the congress and President Ibañez, the congress lifted a state of siege previously declared by the president and managed to maintain its position. On an occasion before this, the congress had declared that Ibañez had an "exaggerated concept of his constitutional prerogative." [2]

Rarely has the impeachment power been exercised against a president while he was in possession of power. In May 1951, President Arnulfo Arías of Panama was convicted after impeachment charges and deprived of the right ever to hold office in the republic. Usually impeachment threats are heard after the president has left office and is actually not accessible to the authorities.

Thus, in the ineffectiveness of the legislative branch, we observe one of the serious defects of Latin American systems with respect to the constitutional prescription of separation of powers. A typical Latin American president, faced with lack of co-operation from the legislative branch, is likely to exhibit considerable impatience. He will occasionally sacrifice a few of his ministers in a show of reshuffling the cabinet to suit congressional opinion, but he is not likely to go a step farther. Very often, of course, his control is secure enough to obviate any substantial opposition. As "co-legislator," he manages the congress as he would a department or ministry.

The Judical Power[3]

The independent judiciary, long a feature of British and North American systems, has not, on the whole, flourished in Latin America. It is perhaps safe to generalize that the judiciary is, in the main, in a less vulnerable position with respect to executive domination than the legislative branch. One does not need to look far to appreciate the subsidiary character of the judiciary in a typical Latin American republic. In addition to the overpowering position of the president, there is a deep-seated tendency to accept judicial activity as a supplementary activity of the general authority to create policy, a result perhaps of the traditional Iberian habit of considering all officialdom as essentially judgeship. In colonial days both the viceroy and *audiencia* were associated with judicial activity. Furthermore, when one considers the general orientation of continental civil law toward the emphasis on the state in the judicial process, the whole picture focuses more clearly.

Structure. The typical Latin American republic provides a judicial structure that falls into the common pattern in use throughout a major part of the world. That is, a three-level system, with minor courts of various types at the local level classified as simple magistrate courts, superior courts established at a district or provincial level, and, finally, a supreme court of the system. Designations vary; a typical set might be: Municipal or Mayor's Court, Superior Court, and Supreme Court of Justice.

Argentina and Mexico have distinctive patterns of courts that follow their federal structure. Thus, in Argentina are found provincial court systems and in Mexico state court systems, in addition to the national judiciary with the complications of jurisdiction that have, for example, characterized the system of courts in the federal system in the United States. It should be observed, however, that, because the national government in each case has been given by constitution powers to create certain national codes (such as commerce and aviation), national jurisdiction tends to be more sweeping than in the United States.

Judges. Judges in Latin America are usually appointed by the president, although other means are sometimes employed, such as congressional appointment. Terms of office vary widely, from four years to life. In addition, the terms for judges of lower courts are usually shorter than those in the supreme court. The Latin American literature on judicial personnel frequently dwells at length on the question of irremovability (*inamovilidad*). In general, the tenor of this is that irremovability ought to prevail for the term of appointment except for serious malfeasance in the performance of duties. The fact that judges are removed or forced to resign by pressure of political circumstance accounts for the great interest in this subject. Impeachment is normally a possible avenue to removal.

Political Involvement of Courts. In much of Latin America, judges are regarded as detached from the most direct forms of political activity. Thus, it occasionally happens that a supreme court justice will be considered a likely personage to act in a provisional capacity while the major political struggle is resolved.

In some cases, it has been clear that the judiciary will make a determined stand against the onslaught of a new regime on the system. Thus, the supreme court of Argentina struck down a number of decrees of President Perón, declaring them unconstitutional. For their efforts, in 1947, most of the justices were impeached, convicted, and removed from their posts by a Peronist-dominated Congress. Impeachment provides a very simple remedy for the president faced by a recalcitrant court, since he will normally be able to command sufficient support from a subservient legislative branch. However, it is usually not necessary to resort to this weapon.

Interestingly enough, in situations where frequent political turbulence destroys the continuity provided by the constitution, the supreme court may be regarded as a vestige of constitutional continuity. The court may be requested to extend legality to an extra-constitutional situation, at least temporarily until the old full continuity of the constitutional provisions may be secured. Thus in Argentina the supreme court has on a number of occasions issued *acordados,* which have been stamps of approval for a *de facto* government.[4]

Judicial Review. Nearly all the republics provide for some degree of judicial review—the power to review legislation

with a view to determining constitutionality or unconstitutionality. The immense influence of the courts in the
United States with respect to this activity is well known;
the Latin American adoption of this technique is largely
attributable to the model of the United States. The effect
of a declaration of unconstitutionality varies in the republics. For example, in some, the effect is the same as in
the United States—that is, the inapplicability of the law in
general. In others, however, the inapplicability is made to
extend only to the particular case causing the judgment.
And, as a practical matter, it occasionally happens that
the executive power will ignore the ruling of the court in
any case (as did Perón in the celebrated impeachment
affair mentioned above).

It appears that judicial review cannot be regarded as a
reliable check on the executive or legislative branches.
Acceptance will always be subject to the willingness or
unwillingness of the executive to accede.

CHAPTER EIGHT

Reflections on the Future of Latin American Government

Literature and speeches on Latin American government throughout the years have stressed the lack of effective democratic systems in many of the republics. This view contains much truth, and it is unnecessary to repeat it. Some observations are helpful, however, in analyzing the nature of the obstacles to effective democratic systems and in properly assessing the future that may be expected.

Institutionally, the problem of change in this direction means a shift of emphasis from executive power to legislative power and also the placing of the center of gravity in practice where it rests in theory—that is, in the hands of the people. Both Latin Americans and foreign observers realize, of course, that mass awareness in itself is meaningless. Thus, enormous changes in the internal socio-economic sphere will have to be accomplished. Also, external problems that relate to national pride and effective foreign relations are involved in the ultimate solution.

Social and Economic Progress

In the internal variable of the state of social and economic well-being lies the most widely acknowledged obstacle to effective political systems in the Latin American world. Latin Americans themselves are just as much in agreement on this point as the outsiders who constantly appraise their futures with pessimism.

It seems fairly well established that the way to effective representative accountability is through the creation of an abundant, or at least a constantly satisfactory, economy. It is perhaps not necessary that the economy be primarily industrial, but it is necessary that the economy be sufficiently diversified so that some degree of self-sufficiency may be expected. When confidence can be created in the "self-starting" type of economy, then there arises the climate for the creation of a local capital formation. A series of self-generating impulses are set up that tend to create a momentum that will carry beyond ordinary economic crisis. The lesson of modern history in the area of Western democratic action seems to be that middle-class solidity and productivity are closely related to orderliness and effectiveness of government; corollaries are social mobility and the possibility of fulfillment of ordinary aspirations. These goals need not be considered crass and lowly; as much loftiness of spirit and creativity in all the refinements of human accomplishment can be expected as in any other society.

Thus, the formula consists of energy, inventiveness, and a conviction that the lifting up of the living standard is not merely useful but desirable. Real economic independence comes from a disposition to change, to educate, to invent, to sell, to produce, and, finally, to dignify all these energies.

The most significant result of Western industrial societies, politically speaking, is that they have created a diversion from political power and, accordingly, have created diffusion rather than focus. In Latin America there is a very great need to build up the power of the consumer, who finds satisfaction in tasting of many diffuse delights, to challenge the power of the ruling cliques, who focus chiefly on the delight of public authority. In short, the pluralism of power—power broken into its components—seems best calculated to introduce responsible systems. In Latin America, this has been assumed as a commitment or an accompaniment to the goal chosen years ago when the revolting colonies joined the company of modern revolutionaries.

Cultural traits appear to adjust easily to such socio-economic changes as would be necessary to create the proper foundation for an effective representative system. If we can judge from experience in the United States, national groups with authoritarian traditions melt into a pluralistic popular system and seem to be as amenable to it as groups said to be in a more democratic tradition. Evidence is indeed strong that much of Latin America today is entering into an essentially middle-class business-man pattern of attitudes and goals. The demands of such an orientation will surely bring about the development that has been observed in the established systems, such as in the United States. There will be a demand for skilled workmen, a large, trained managerial group, thousands of clerical workers, and the other components of an active inter-dependent industrial order. These will shift the center of gravity. They will undertake a dual power thrust, observable in the already established systems of this type: the center of gravity in political power and the center of gravity in the economic system as an enormous internal consumer force.

What a market awaits the economy in a typical Latin American republic that adequately gears for the internal needs! There will have to be, of course, forceful and intelligent management of the capital-formation phase of this development. This does not necessarily mean private capitalism, although this latter will undoubtedly be a more attractive incentive for foreign capital investment. But, once the development is underway, millions of inadequately housed and otherwise ill-equipped Latin American families will provide a market that staggers the imagination.

A number of concessions will have to be made. First of all, in those republics where valuable lands are wastefully held in antiquated and inefficient production, the land-holders must sell, lease, or otherwise open these lands to production. Secondly, the educational system will have to provide larger numbers of nonprofessional skills; the traditional aim of the educated groups must be changed, at least partly, from the law-medicine-politics alignment to the engineer-entrepreneur alignment. Thirdly, the military must shift its emphasis from guardianship in the political sense to strict professionalism, with emphasis on engineering and science. Fourthly, Latin Americans must move into their own exploratory and inventive operations in order to encourage foreign capital instead of relying on foreign teams to supply the whole development; that is, they must present the attractive venture rather than merely witness it.

In many parts of Latin America, this whole prospect is regarded with distaste. It is said to be potentially destructive of the cultural values of the society. There is a tendency to point to the history of the United States as illustrating rather more profit-consciousness than spiritual values. There is no point in debating this issue here. It might be well to stress, however, that the cultural values of Latin American societies can be achieved with the brilliance and tastefulness native to those societies. There is every promise that the future Latin American socio-economic order may be loftily inspired as well as productive.

Effective Nationalism

An important factor in the total political pattern of Latin America is small-state nationalism, with its many defensive characteristics. The relations of many republics with the

United States—and the resulting anti-Yankee attitudes—are prominent examples of this position. Such positions are unfortunately deterrents to effectiveness in the general political sense. But the fact must be faced that the republics are small units living in a world dominated by titans who draft the rules. The adoption of some effective means of living with this fact should engage the attentions of Latin American leaders rather more than insistence on dwelling upon this matter emotionally.

It might be pointed out that the Latin American republics have performed admirably and expertly in international life—in the League of Nations, the United Nations, specialized international agencies, and in the Organization of American States. They have worked vigorously and enthusiastically to accomplish the traditional goals of small nations. Representatives of Latin American republics are well oriented in the direction of such work, with its emphasis upon the upgrading of small nations to some position of equality and upon idealism in world order.

In the past, it was possible for the small European nation to hold its own through colonial ventures or by skillfully finding a place in the industrial order. The latter is certainly a possibility for most Latin American republics. But the former course is denied them. This is one of the penalties that history has placed upon new nations, which have jumped into the game too late to assist in the drafting of the rules.

There is very great promise—in theory—in a number of Latin American confederations. Although at the present the actuality appears impossible—even in that part of Middle America where such a confederation was once a reality—the advantages of such action would be tremendous. It may be that with the mellowness of nationalism that inevitably accompanies an improvement in the socio-economic base more consideration may be given to this possibility. If it could be arranged—one, two, or several confederations—Latin America could eventually enter the game on terms of equality or near-equality. The difficulties of confederation are well known. Even in the United States, where confederation was almost natural, a furious war disrupted the scheme for a time. But who knows what the cultural uniformity of Latin America may be able to accomplish in this respect, when conditions now conducive to excessive nationalism change, lessen, or perhaps disappear?

Constitutions and Reality

Inevitably, after an appraisal of Latin American political institutions and activity, the gap between constitutional prescription and practice is expressed in very pessimistic terms. This appraisal is certainly justified in regard to the past or the present. There is, however, a future that appears promising.

It is no longer realistic to describe Latin American political institutions as alien plants in unpromising soil, slavish copies of other models. As we have seen, institutions themselves can become environmental influences. By a revolutionary commitment too strong to ignore, Latin America adopted a set of institutions which—barring some extraordinary new commitment—will in time square with reality. There are signs that much of the gap has already been closed in a number of the republics.

All modern constitutional systems have a job of fulfillment, a gap to close. The British system is regarded as a marvel among nations because it proceeded to develop the substance of a thing before the expression of it. But such is not given to all modern republics, coming into existence as they have, in other circumstances. Even in the United States, where, it may be said, the British system continued to develop in many respects, some problem of fulfillment can be found. Thus, it may be argued that the revolutionary commitment of the United States to full and complete civil rights has not been in fact fully fulfilled, particularly if one regards the Declaration of Independence as a binding moral supplement to the Constitution.

One is of course strongly tempted to blueprint a set of institutions that would suit the pattern observable at the moment, together with the possible future development of this pattern. Besides being too risky, such a draft is likely not to fit all the situations presented throughout Latin America. My own opinion is that the strong-president system will not be substantially altered. If a shift of emphasis from executive to legislative power takes place, it is unlikely that a responsible cabinet system will evolve in many republics. Curiously, there is greater likelihood that a paternalistic cabinet system (such as that recently erected in France around General de Gaulle) might evolve. Interestingly enough, if this should develop it would represent an arrival at a midpoint, the French by way of an assembly-dominated approach and the Latin American by way of a president-dominated approach.

Chapter 1. THE IBERIAN HERITAGE

1. The best survey on the colonial system in English: C. H. Haring, *The Spanish Empire in America,* New York, 1947.

2. S. E. Morison, *Admiral of the Ocean Sea,* Boston, 1942.

3. Roscoe R. Hill, "The Office of Adelantado," *Political Science Quarterly,* XXVIII, 4 (December 1913), 646-68.

4. *Ibid.,* pp. 657-62.

5. In *South America,* New York, 1912, p. 534.

6. Bartolomé Mitre, *Ensayos históricos,* Buenos Aires, 1939, p. 76.

7. See W. L. Schurz in *The Evolution of Latin American Government,* ed. A. N. Christensen, New York, 1951, pp. 12-52.

8. C. H. Cunningham, *The* Audiencia *in the Spanish Colonies,* Berkeley, 1919.

9. W. W. Pierson, Jr., "Some Reflections on the *Cabildo* as an Institution," *Hispanic American Historical Review,* V, 4 (November 1922), 573-96.

10. J. Lloyd Mecham, *Church and State in Latin America,* Chapel Hill, 1934.

11. See one of the classics of the colonial system: Solórzano y Perreyra, *Política Indiana,* 5 vols., Madrid, 1930.

12. Alexander von Humboldt, *Political Essay on the Kingdom of New Spain,* London, 1822, I, 8; herein Humboldt refers to nine separate kingdoms.

13. Crane Brinton, *The Anatomy of Revolution,* New York, 1938, Ch. 2.

14. Bernard Moses, *The Intellectual Background of the Revolution in South America,* New York, 1926.

15. H. F. Peterson, "Mariano Moreno: The Making of an Insurgent," *Hispanic American Historical Review,* XIV, 4 (November 1934), 450-76.

16. Quoted in Ricardo Rojas, *El Pensamiento de Sarmiento,* Buenos Aires, 1941, p. 190.

17. V. A. Belaunde, *Bolívar and the Political Thought of the Spanish American Revolution,* Baltimore, 1938, pp. 1388-89.

18. J. B. Alberdi, *Bases y puntos de partida para la organización política de la República Argentina,* Buenos Aires, 1943, p. 56, offers this quotation.

19. Moses, *op. cit,* pp. 155-56, quotes this remark.

20. A. C. Wilgus (ed.), *South American Dictators: During the First Century of Independence,* Washington, D. C., 1937.

Chapter 2. CONSTITUTIONS AND GENERAL STRUCTURE

1. Russell H. Fitzgibbon, "Constitutional Development in Latin America: A Synthesis," *American Political Science Review,* XXXIX, 3 (June 1945), 511-22.

2. Gabriel Storni, *Suspensión de las garantías constitucionales,* Santa Fe, Argentina, 1945; see also Clinton Rossiter, *Constitutional Dictatorship,* Princeton, 1948, Ch. 6.

3. George I. Blanksten, *Ecuador: Constitutions and Caudillos,* Berkeley and Los Angeles, 1951, pp. 170-71.

4. Russell H. Fitzgibbon, *"Continuismo* in Central America and the Caribbean," *Inter-American Quarterly,* II, 3 (July 1940), 55-74.

Chapter 3. THE ELECTORAL PROCESS

1. "The Development of Democracy on the American Continent," *American Political Science Review,* XVI, 1 (February 1922), 3.

2. See Russell H. Fitzgibbon, "A Statistical Evaluation of Latin American Democracy," *Western Political Quarterly,* IX, 3 (September 1956), 607-19; also, W. W. Pierson (ed.), "Pathology of Democracy in Latin America: A Symposium," *American Political Science Review,* XLIV, 1 (March 1950), 100-49.

3. United Nations, Department of Social Affairs, *Preliminary Report on the World Social Situation,* New York, 1952, p. 4.

4. Pan American Union, Office of Social Sciences, *Materials for the Study of the Middle Class in Latin America*, Washington, D. C., 1950.

5. See George I. Blanksten, "Political Groups in Latin America," *American Political Science Review*, LIII, 1 (March 1959), 106-27; also, Russell H. Fitzgibbon, "The Party Potpourri in Latin America," *Western Political Quarterly*, X, 1 (March 1957), 3-22.

6. George I. Blanksten, *Perón's Argentina*, Chicago, 1953.

7. R. S. Abbott, "The Role of Contemporary Political Parties in Chile," *American Political Science Review*, XLV, 2 (June 1951), 450-63.

8. R. H. Fitzgibbon, *Uruguay: Portrait of a Democracy*, New Brunswick, N. J., 1954.

9. L. Vincent Padgett, "Mexico's One-Party System: A Re-evaluation," *American Political Science Review*, LI, 4 (December 1957), 995-1008.

10. J. Lloyd Mecham, *Church and State in Latin America*, Chapel Hill, 1934.

11. Robert J. Alexander, *Labor Movements in Latin America*, London, 1947.

12. Frank R. Brandenburg, in *Government and Politics in Latin America*, ed. H. E. Davis, New York, 1958, Ch. 8.

Chapter 4. REVOLUTION, VIOLENCE, POLITICAL MORALITY

1. Reported in New York *Times*, July 27, 1949, at 13/1.

2. See Robert J. Alexander, in *Government and Politics in Latin America*, ed. H. E. Davis, New York, 1958, Ch. 6.

3. *Bases y puntos de partida . . . ,* Buenos Aires, 1943, p. 45.

4. Majid Khadduri, "The Role of the Military in Middle East Politics," *American Political Science Review,* XLVII, 2 (June 1953), 511-24.

5. Reported in New York *Times,* November 5, 1948, at 12/3.

6. *Ibid.,* April 4, 1954, at 24/1, following the *coup* of June 1953.

7. *Ibid.,* August 25, 1949, at 12/5.

8. Alona E. Evans, "The Colombian-Peruvian Asylum Case: The Practice of Diplomatic Asylum," *American Political Science Review,* XLVI, 1 (March 1952), 142-57.

9. *Latin America: Its Rise and Progress,* London, 1919, p. 31.

10. See William S. Stokes, "Violence as a Power Factor in Latin American Politics," *Western Political Quarterly,* V, 3 (September 1952), 445-68.

Chapter 5. THE EXECUTIVE POWER

1. *An Essay on the True Principles of Executive Power in the Great States,* 2 vols., London, 1792, I, 1.

2. Karl Loewenstein, "The Presidency Outside the United States: A Study in Comparative Political Institutions," *Journal of Politics,* II, 3 (August 1949), 447-96.

3. Milton I. Vanger, "Uruguay Introduces Government by Committee," *American Political Science Review,* XLVIII, 2 (June 1954), 500-13.

4. William S. Stokes, "Parliamentary Government in Latin America," *American Political Science Review,* XXXIX, 3 (June 1945), 522-36.

5. R. A. Gomez, "Intervention in Argentina, 1869-1930," *Inter-American Economic Affairs*, I, 3 (December 1947), 55-73.

6. Alberto R. Real, *Los decretos-leyes*, Montevideo, 1946.

Chapter 6. PRESIDENTS, *CAUDILLOS*, AND GUARDIANS

1. Karl Loewenstein has been emphatic on this point on several occasions, See his *Brazil under Vargas*, New York, 1942, p. 450, for example.

2. For a good series of reports on the National Revolutionary Movement in Bolivia, see the letters of Richard W. Patch for the American Universities Field Staff, particularly "Bolivia: the Seventh Year," February 3, 1959, and "Bolivian Background," October 10, 1958.

3. Russell H. Fitzgibbon, *"Continuismo* in Central America and the Caribbean," *Inter-American Quarterly*, XI, 3 (July 1940), 55-74.

4. Russell H. Fitzgibbon, "A Statistical Evaluation of Latin-American Democracy," *Western Political Quarterly*, IX, 3 (September, 1956), 607-19.

5. George I. Blanksten, *Perón's Argentina*, Chicago, 1953.

6. New York *Times*, October 31, 1948, at 38/4.

7. New York, 1938, p. 232.

Chapter 7. THE SUBSIDIARY LEGISLATIVE AND JUDICIAL POWERS

1. See Robert E. Scott, in *Government and Politics in Latin America*, ed. H. E. Davis, New York, 1958, Ch. 11.

2. New York *Times*, December 17, 1954, at 7/1.

3. Helen L. Clagett, *The Administration of Justice in Latin America,* New York, 1952.

4. J. I. Puente, "The Nature and Powers of a 'De Facto' Government in Latin America," *Tulane Law Review,* XXX (1955).

BIBLIOGRAPHICAL NOTE

The Latin American area in the field of government and politics is not blessed with a long list of titles that explore either theory or practice sufficiently to give a wealth of background to students. It must be said, however, that remarkable gains have been made in this direction in the last fifteen years. In somewhat more than half of the twenty republics there now exists some foundation at least for the pursuance of more detailed work. Latin Americanists, particularly in the United States, are becoming more active and—most significant—are beginning to approach their studies with some support from hitherto untapped research funds. Obviously, "the classic" in Latin American politics, if it is ever written at all, will inevitably have to be an enormous work to appraise properly the systems of twenty republics. But some first class works on single republics, or on some segments of the area of politics broadly conceived throughout Latin America, have been written and more undoubtedly are on the way.

The following titles are selected with a view to their particular usefulness in political science. Many have been omitted that would be indispensable for detailed study. Not included, for example, are a large number of articles in such professional journals as *American Political Science Review* and *Western Political Quarterly*, other political science publications, and journals in the disciplines of history, philosophy, sociology, and economics.

GENERAL

G. Arciniegas. *The State of Latin America*. New York, Alfred A. Knopf, 1952.

James Bryce. *South America*. New York, Macmillan, 1912.

A. N. Christensen (ed.). *The Evolution of Latin American Government*. New York, Henry Holt, 1951.

W. Rex Crawford. *A Century of Latin American Thought*. Cambridge, Harvard University Press, 1944.

Harold E. Davis (ed.). *Government and Politics in Latin America*. New York, Ronald, 1958.

A. F. Macdonald. *Latin American Politics and Government*. 2d ed. New York, Thomas Y. Crowell, 1954.

J. Lloyd Mecham. *Church and State in Latin America*. Chapel Hill, N. C., University of North Carolina Press, 1934.

William W. Pierson and Federico G. Gil. *Governments of Latin America*. New York, McGraw-Hill, 1957.

William L. Schurz. *Latin America: A Descriptive Survey*. New York, E. P. Dutton, 1942.

Stanford University. Hispanic American Studies. *Hispanic American Report* (monthly).

ARGENTINA

Robert J. Alexander. *The Perón Era.* New York, Columbia University Press, 1951.

George I. Blanksten. *Perón's Argentina.* Chicago, University of Chicago Press, 1953.

A. F. Macdonald. *Government of the Argentine Republic.* New York, Thomas Y. Crowell, 1942.

Ysabel F. Rennie. *The Argentine Republic.* New York, Macmillan, 1945.

Carl C. Taylor. *Rural Life in Argentina.* Baton Rouge, Louisiana State University Press, 1948.

BOLIVIA

Harold Osborne. *Bolivia: A Land Divided.* London, Royal Institute of International Affairs, 1954.

Richard W. Patch. Series of Letters for American Universities Field Service. 1958, 1959.

BRAZIL

Ernest Hambloch. *His Majesty the President of Brazil.* New York, E. P. Dutton, 1936.

Karl Loewenstein. *Brazil under Vargas.* New York, Macmillan, 1942.

T. Lynn Smith. *Brazil: People and Institutions.* Rev. ed. Baton Rouge, Louisiana State University Press, 1955.

CHILE

Gilbert J. Butland. *Chile: An Outline of Its Geography, Economics and Politics.* London, Royal Institute of International Affairs, 1951.

Ricardo Donoso. *Desarollo político y social de Chile desde la Constitución de 1833*. Santiago de Chile, Imprenta Universitaria, 1942.

————. *Las Ideas políticas en Chile*. Mexico, Fondo de Cultura Económica, 1946.

John R. Stevenson. *The Popular Front in Chile*. Philadelphia, University of Pennsylvania Press, 1942.

COLOMBIA

W. O. Galbraith. *Colombia: A General Survey*. London, Royal Institute of International Affairs, 1953.

G. Sánchez Gómez. *Sociología Política Colombiana*. Calí, Colombia, Sánchez Gómez Hnos., 1943.

COSTA RICA

John and Mavis Biesanz. *Costa Rican Life*. New York, Columbia University Press, 1944.

Harry Kantor. *The Costa Rican Election of 1953*. Gainesville, University of Florida Press, 1958.

Stacy May *et al. Costa Rica*. New York, The Twentieth Century Fund, 1952.

ECUADOR

George I. Blanksten. *Ecuador: Constitutions and* Caudillos. Berkeley and Los Angeles, University of California Press, 1951.

GUATEMALA

K. H. Silvert. *A Study in Government: Guatemala*. Part I. New Orleans, Middle America Research Institute, Tulane University, 1954.

————. *A Study in Government: Guatemala.* Part II. New Orleans, Middle America Research Institute, Tulane University, 1956.

HONDURAS

W. S. Stokes. *Honduras: An Area Study in Government.* Madison, University of Wisconsin Press, 1950.

MEXICO

Patrick Romanell. *The Making of the Mexican Mind.* Lincoln, University of Nebraska Press, 1952.

J. Silva Herzog. *La Revolución Mexicana en crisis.* Mexico, Ediciones Cuadernos Americanos, 1944.

Frank Tannenbaum. *Mexico: The Struggle for Peace and Bread.* New York, Knopf, 1950.

W. P. Tucker. *Mexican Government Today.* Minneapolis, University of Minnesota Press, 1957.

Nathan L. Whetten. *Rural Mexico.* Chicago, University of Chicago Press, 1948.

PERU

Harry Kantor. *The Ideology and Program of the Peruvian Aprista Movement.* Berkeley, University of California Press, 1953.

T. R. Ford. *Man and Land in Peru.* Gainesville, University of Florida Press, 1955.

URUGUAY

Russell H. Fitzgibbon. *Uruguay: Portrait of a Democracy.* New Brunswick, Rutgers University Press, 1954.

Simon G. Hanson. *Utopia in Uruguay*. New York, Oxford University Press, 1938.

VENEZUELA

L. Vallenilla Lanz. *Cesarismo democrático*. Carácas, Empresa El Cojo, 1919.